AF209699

BOARD N'STONES

Acknowledgements

My thanks go to Christian N. for his technical support on AI setup and maintenance.
Many thanks as well to Max for his support in reviewing the book!

March 2021, Gunnar Dickfeld

GUNNAR DICKFELD

SEVEN

THE GO SUPER MATCH

SHIN JINSEO VS PARK JUNGHWAN

BOARD N'STONES

The German National Library lists this publication in the Deutsche National-bibliografie; detailed bibliographic data are available in the Internet at https://dnb.dnb.de.

ISBN 978-3-940563-79-8

© 2021, BOARD N'STONES, Gunnar Dickfeld, Frankfurt a.M.
BOARD N'STONES is a trademark of Brett und Stein Verlag

Cover design: Lars Decker
Print: Books on Demand GmbH, Norderstedt

 The diagrams in this book were created with
SmartGo™: http://www.smartgo.com

The Beautiful Treasure Island Namhae
Shin Jinseo vs. Park Junghwan
Baduk Super Match

The „Beautiful Treasure Island Namhae Shin Jinseo vs Park Junghwan Baduk Super Match" has been a highlight in the go world, not only in Korea but also worldwide. Korea's top two players, 1st ranked Shin Jinseo 9p and 2nd ranked Park Junghwan 9p, were seeded to play a match of seven games. Each of these games were played in selected locations around the beautiful Namhae island, the major island of Namhae county in South Gyeongsang Province. This event was characterized by the combination of scenic and cultural landmarks and the highest level of Korea's human go players.

The first game of the Super Match series took place on October 19th and the last on December 2nd 2020. The venues for the tournament were situated across Namhae island, where beautiful sites were chosen as stages for each of the individual games: the Gwaneumru pavilion, Sangju Eunmore Beach, the German village, the Namhae Bridge, the Nodo Island of Literature, the Seolri Skywalk, and the Namhae Exile Literature Museum.

The event was sponsored by Namhae county. Jang Chung-nam, the head of Namhae County, has a close relationship with Shin Jinseo's father, both having grown up in the same town called Daegok-ri, Namhae. When Shin Jinseo became a world class go player, interest in go increased among the people of Namhae. So, Jang thought that despite the county's limited financial resources, it would be a great idea to bring Shin Jinseo and Park Junghwan to Namhae for the benefit of the local people, to promote their amazing island and its special products throughout the country, and of course for the benefit of the global go community.

At the opening ceremony of the Super Match, Namhae County Head Jang Chung-nam said, „The world's citizens are suffering from Covid-19. In the midst of this, it makes a lot of sense to hold a Super Match on Namhae, the South Sea treasure island of Korea. Especially the games of world class professionals will give great hope to many citizens, residents of Gyeongsangnam-do, and go enthusiasts worldwide."

Before the Super Match started, both players said they didn't see this competition as a confrontation between two top Korean players, but they promised to play their best go. Shin Jinseo said, „I am grateful to the many people who worked hard to make this event possible, and especially to the head of Namhae County. To honour holding such a wonderful tournament, I will work hard myself and present the best go, this way I want to contribute to the success of the tournament by providing beautiful games." Park Junghwan, after crediting Namhae County and everyone involved in the tournament organization, said: „Shin Jinseo is at the peak of the current go season. It seems like a great opportunity to learn something." He promised to show good games of go.

The Super Match was declared to be a tournament of seven games, where all have to be played irrespective their outcome. They are counted as official competition games and allow the winner of each game to receive 15 million Won (about 11,000 EUR / 13,000 USD). The loser was to receive 5 million Won (about 3,700 EUR / 4,400 USD) per game. For thinking time, each player is given 90 minutes main time plus five periods of one minute byoyomi.

The Super Match confirmed that the throne of the Korean go world has passed from Park Junghwan to Shin Jinseo. Shin Jinseo, who was in competition with Park Junghwan for the top spot since the year before, had reached number one in the go rankings in January 2020.

However, the go world was hesitant to give him the title of "Number One" as he couldn't properly surpass Park Junghwan. In 2019 Shin Jinseo was far behind Park Junghwan with a 4-15 win/loss record. Shin Jinseo was defeated by Park Junghwan in the final of the 2nd Yongseong Battle and the Masters of Baduk TV. But this year, in 2020, the relationship between the two has reversed.

Shin Jinseo defeated Park Junghwan 2-0 in the final of the LG Cup in February and won his first major world championship, followed by defeating Park Junghwan 3-0 in the 1st Korean Strongest Players tournament. In addition he won the 3rd Korean Yongseong, beating Park 2-0. These were five wins in a row for Shin Jinseo against Park Junghwan, summing to a total of 8-1 before the Super Match. Of course, Park Junghwan is an excellent player showing strong results in many tournaments. Therefore, they have established as a pair of rivals. At the time of writing, Shin Jinseo's performance in 2020 was 81-10, a winning rate of about 90%.

In fact, before the Namhae Super Match, most of the go world predicted that no matter who wins, the tournament would likely result in a split of 4-3 or 5-2. Instead, the outcome of the competition was Shin Jinseo's one-sided victory. Namhae Super Match referee Baek Sung-ho 9p said: „Park Junghwan may have lost a lot to Shin Jinseo lately, but he still shows overwhelming ability against other professionals."

With his 7-0 win against Park Junghwan in the Namhae Super Match, Shin Jinseo established himself as „Number One" in terms of win record and rank. This book tells the story of these seven games.

* * *

This book is somewhat of an experiment, which was enabled by the rise of Artificial Intelligence (AI) in the world of go. There is a tradition that game commentaries have long been provided by professionals only. In the western world strong amateurs then began, often based on professional input, to provide commentaries on pro games. Today, given the availability of AI, any amateur can review professional games in a new way. However, they may still need guidance from stronger players in order to elaborate on the hidden aspects which even an AI may not clearly reveal.

The presentation of the games in this book is based on available game commentaries by professionals who have been supported by one AI or another. In many cases it's not clear which AI has actually been used. I added my own research, done with the most popular open source AI today, KataGo, to create an easily digested presentation of the games.

Throughout the book I draw no distinctions between the various AIs, their types and versions, which have with or without credit contributed to the commentaries, and will just refer to „the AI". Like humans, AI's may disagree with each other. Hence, I took the approach to take the average of their final score estimation in case they differed slightly. Where they differed by a lot, I gave preference to one of them based mostly on my own subjective reasoning.

AI's analyse several moves and pick one of them as the preferred, just like humans do. The rejected moves may only be slightly inferior, by fractions of a digit in the estimated final score. These inferior moves may not necessarily be bad ones. Having said this, it should be clear that AI's still allow for a lot of liberty in playing, allowing us to make different choices, explore our own paths, and deploy our own styles. You will see how the two Korean top players adopt modern moves and at the same time discard some of the post AI joseki. The result of such liberty in playing is a variety of different and unique games. However, in some situations the wrong choice of a move can turn the game. Here, the use of AI analysis helps to identify these dramatic moments of a game.

This book provides variation diagrams, but in low numbers. So, not every question the reader may have will be answered with the accompanying diagrams. The reader should not just take note of the diagrams given, but be encouraged to activate his own thinking. Furthermore, I recommend the reader to replay the games on a proper board. This may sound old-school, but it's still an acknowledged method of successful learning. Take your time to enjoy these games!

Contents

ONE

● **Shin Jinseo**   ○ **Park Junghwan**

Date: 2020/10/19
Venue: Gwaneum-ru Pavillion, Yi Sunshin Sunguk Park
Time: 90 min plus 5 × 1 min, Komi: 6.5

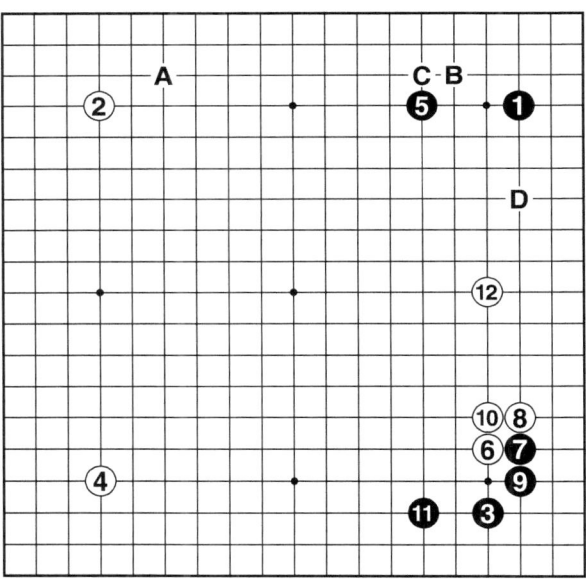

(1 – 12)

5   In pre AI times the approach at A was a modern move, while the
     even more traditional way was building a shimari at B. Before AI,
     Park himself chose to play A in two of his games against Shin.
     Nowadays, the main choices are split between the two large
     shimari 5 and C, but the regular shimari at B is also back in use.

6   This is a common approach to the corner. The low approach
     would be possible here as well.

12   The high extension is a common move to settle this joseki and
     enable a follow up extension at D, which would at the same
     time be an approach to the shimari on the upper side. The low
     extension is rarely seen in this position.

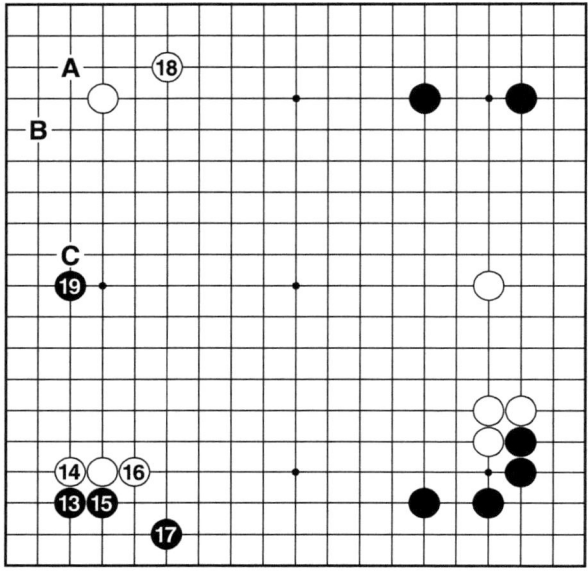

(13 – 19)

13 There is no preference shown by AI towards which 3-3 invasion, A or 13, should be played here. Either is fine.

14 Both sides are good to block, with AI giving a slight preference for the actual move played. See the variation for blocking at 15.

16 This is a simple way to finish the corner and take sente.

18 AI's influence has made this shimari very popular, which is a big change from recent practice. White protects his only corner in this game. Occupying a point like 19 on the left side does not comply with modern opening play anymore. In the past it was common sense to extend from the wall in the lower corner.

19 A good point to prevent a white move here. B or C would also be reasonable moves to establish a base on the left side.

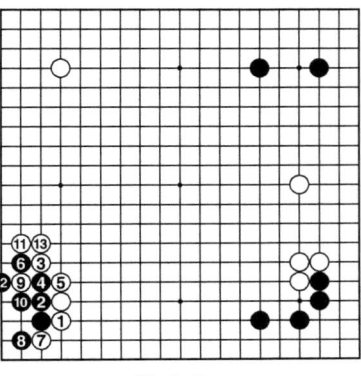

Variation

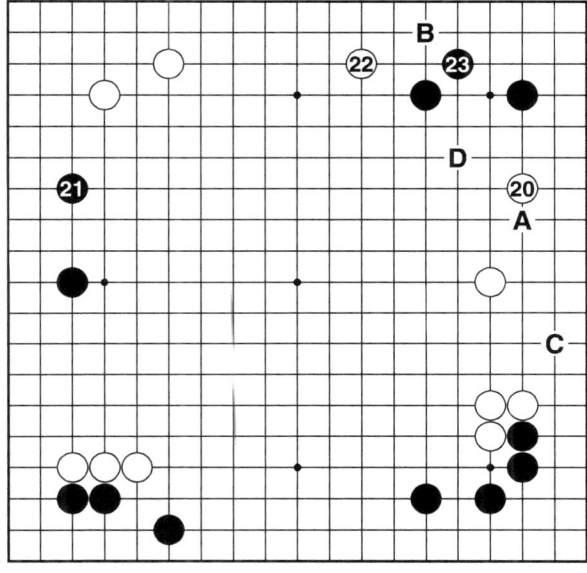

(20 – 23)

20 White is happy to take the extension on the right hand side.
    If White plays the approach at 22 first, Black will not defend at
    B but instead play the checking extension at A. It's probable that
    Park did not like that scenario.

21 Very peaceful move establishing a sound base on the left.
    Black is not waiting for White to take the initiative here and
    force Black into one direction or another. AI also considers the
    immediate invasion at C. However, the difference is marginal.
    So the choice seems a matter of taste or style. Shin opts for a
    peaceful development.

22 Biggest point now.

23 Interesting defensive move, but it is not unique as it has been
    seen in other professional games already. The common move
    to protect the corner here is B. Shin may not have liked that
    White could play the keima at D to force Black to add another
    defensive move.
    After the double approach from two sides, the choice of kosumi
    may in the future become established as a new way to defend
    the large corner enclosure.

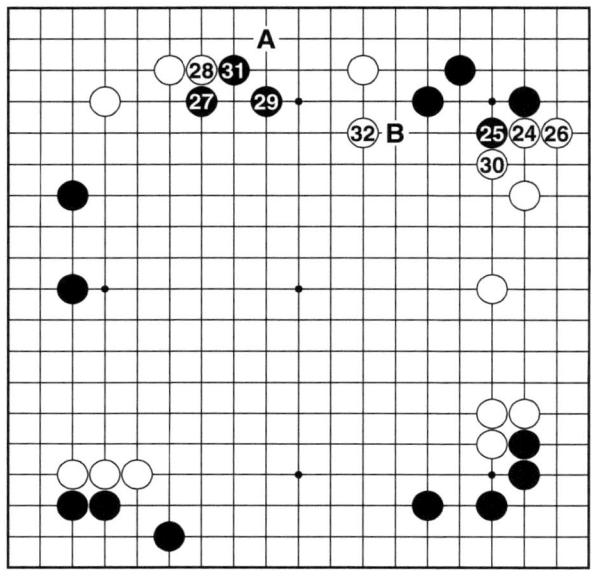

(24 – 32)

24 As the corner cannot be invaded anymore, White plays the contact move from the outside. He wants to make Black over-concentrated and at the same time make his own side thicker.

25 If Black just extends to the edge, the exchange would be good for White. Hence Black is not going to play this way.

27 Black doesn't protect the corner territory, avoiding to invest too many stones here. The group has sufficient shape already. Instead he chooses an active play: the shoulder hit against the shimari.

30 White at A would be a normal continuation, but White ignores that to play the tiger mouth instead.

31 Black ignores White as well.

32 White jumps out to separate the groups. This is a bit heavy. White should play the keima at B, allowing a follow up as in the variation. He shouldn't be worried that Black would push at A and cut.

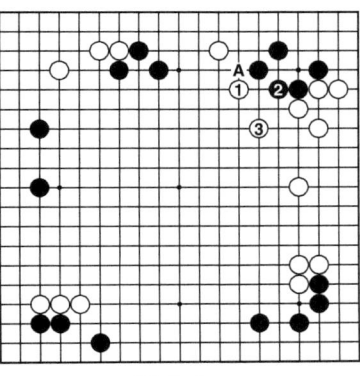

Variation

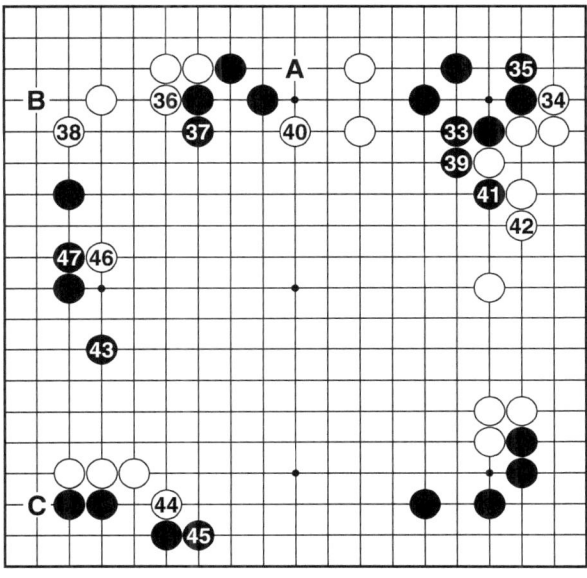

(33 – 47)

33 Black comes back to reinforce his corner group.

34 AI analysis prefers to omit this exchange to instead help the group at the top with A. At this point Black has a very small lead.

38 This move is protecting the corner against a large keima at B.

40 Park decides to support his group. AI still prefers A.

42 Connecting would be too slow. Even more, Black may take advantage of the remaining weakness and attach at 4 in the variation.

43 If Black would jump one line further down it would trigger tougher action by White against the corner, e.g. beginning with C. This may not fit into Black's plan for a large-scale attack.

44 Necessary exchange to help the three stones. This exchange could also have been played earlier, e.g. before 18.

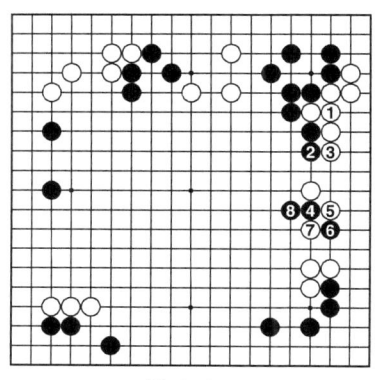

Variation

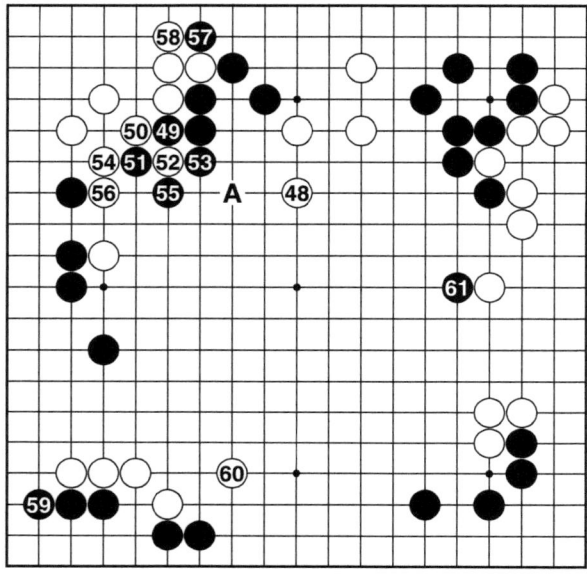

(48 – 61)

48　AI analysis has shown that this move is a slight loss. Common feeling would be attaching at 56. White is probably worried that Black can press harder with A against White's group. At this point Black leads by about two points.

49　Black aims at sealing White in, as shown in the variation. Black's position would get very thick and White may not really try to escape with the cutting stone by extending to A.

50　White cannot play at 56 anymore, as Black would ignore to push at 50. This move aims at exploiting the weakness in the corner.

52　White decides to sacrifice a single stone to prevent Black from connecting.

61　Black feels an invasion at the side to no longer be possible due to the strong position above. Hence he probes with the attachment. This may also be seen as a preparation for attacking the center group.

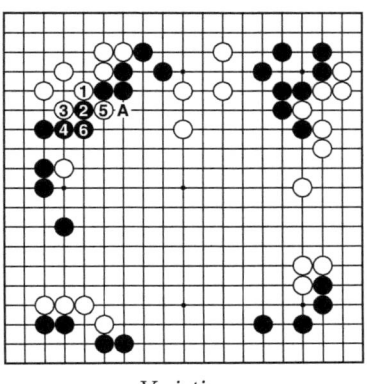

Variation

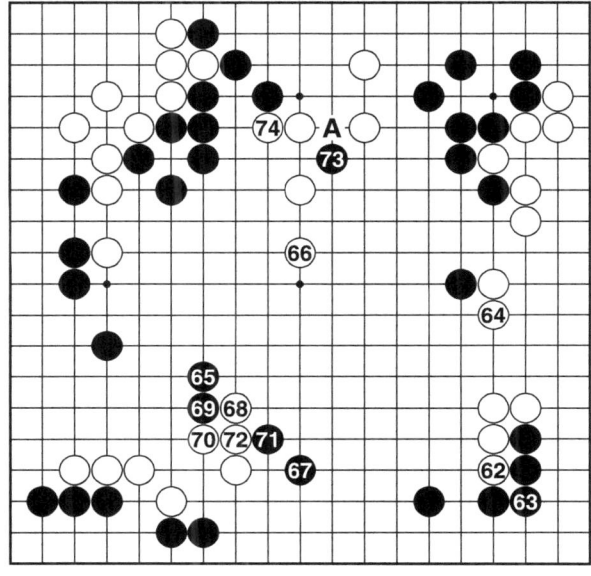

(62 – 74)

65   This is an interesting move in the center. It aims at attacking both of White's groups. Just taking solid territory at the bottom is not good enough for Black. The lower side is not so valuable right now.

73   This move is a probe to see how White will answer. It was a big surprise for the game observers that Shin actually hit the move the AI was recommending. In the variation, White connects at 1. He doesn't need to be afraid of Black 2.

74   White doesn't simply want to be forced to connect. Hence he plays a move which also threatens Black's eye shape before connecting at A.

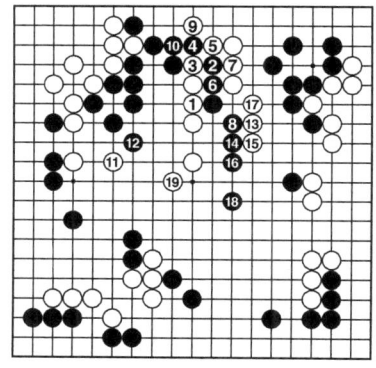

Variation

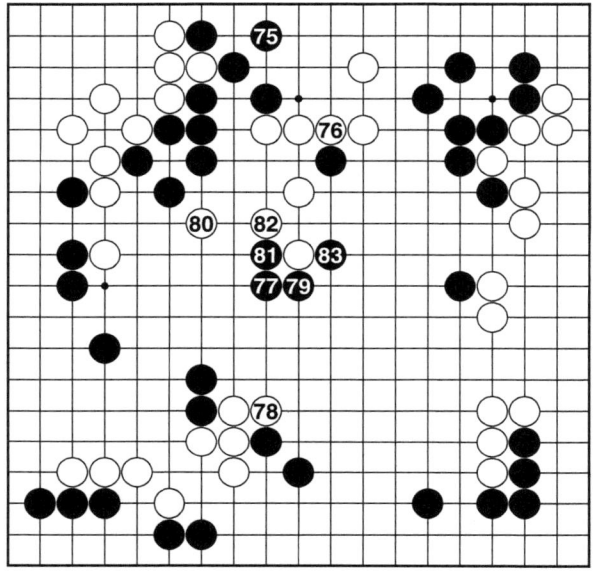

(75 – 83)

77 Black now has sente to attack the lower white group, aiming at separating the two groups from each other.

80 White is also keen on separating Black's groups.

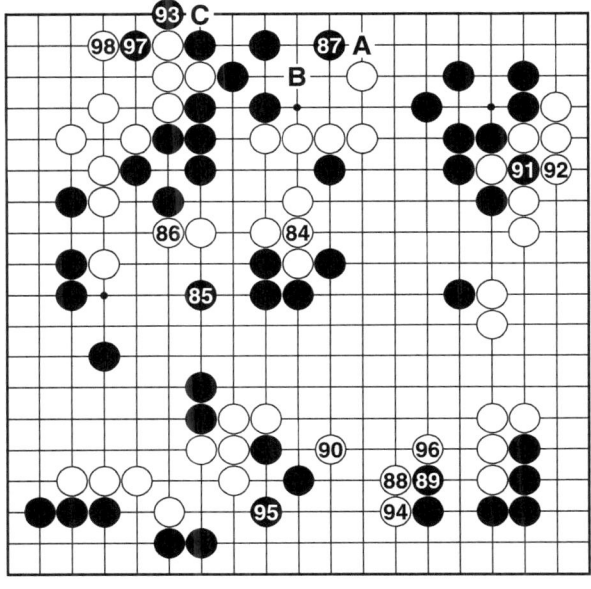

(84 – 98)

84 It looks very painful if White doesn't connect the atari at 83, but actually AI does not agree. White should immediately play 86 to link up his own groups.

85 Black misses the opportunity to play 86 himself, which would have been a strong move. Instead, Black intends to build thickness in the center, aiming at an attack against the lower white group.

87 Black secures eye shape for his group.

88 White plays tenuki. It seems he did not see the value in blocking at A, a sente move which would seal Black in and force him to live locally. If Black answers at B, White would get C in sente as well. However, White plays 88 and 90 to reduce Black's position on the lower side and and at the same time to prepare an escape route to the right for the white group on the left side.

91 Black captures a stone. This kikashi was playable any time.

93 Black increases his territory with an almost sente move.

94 Park ignores 93 to continue at the bottom and link up his group.

98 Now, White needs to answer of course.

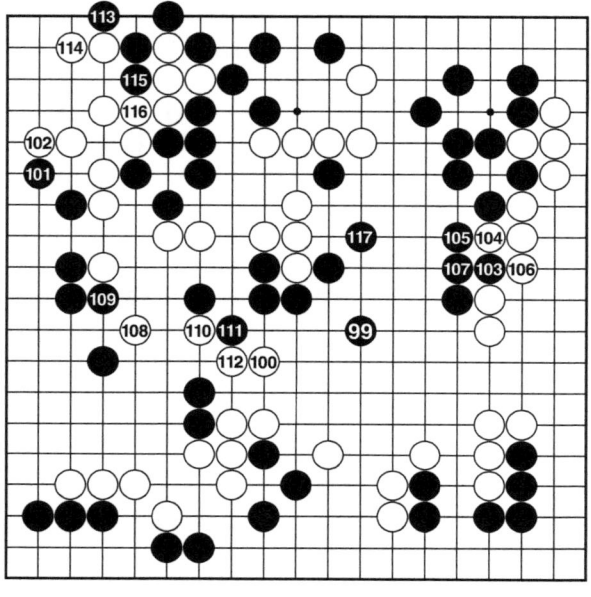

(99 – 117)

99 At this stage of the game Black plays a series of early endgame moves solidifying his current lead. Black is now ahead by about four points.

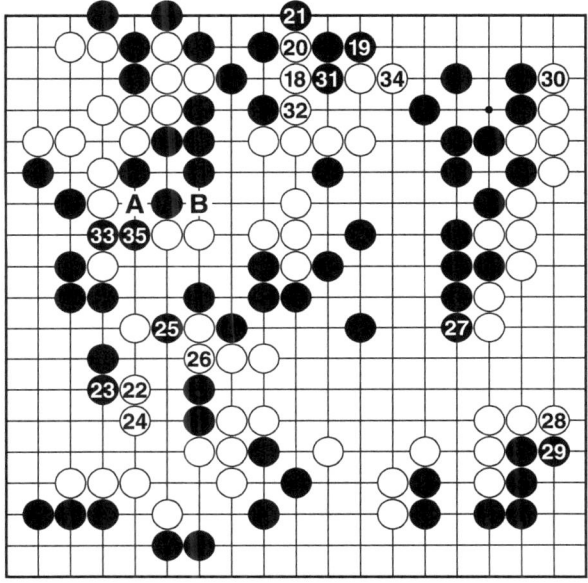

(118 – 135)

127 This move seems rather small and is counted by AI analysis as a loss of two points. It would better to play the hane at 128 and connect at 129.

133 This is a mistake! There is no reason here to atari the stone. It's not attractive anymore to separate the white groups. Black should simply gain solid eye shape for his own group with A instead. This would turn all the points at the top into territory. Due to this mistake Black's shape is thin and will be squeezed to zero points of territory. Even worse, Black will end up needing to sacrifice some of his stones at the top.
The observers were very surprised to see this move played. They did not expect such a mistake by Shin. Black should have simply played A and then B to make a secure eye.

134 White takes advantage of this mistake and extends. Black will be forced to connect on the second line here. If not immediately, then later.

135 Another doubtful move. It's still better to take A or B. B is also a threat to cut off White.

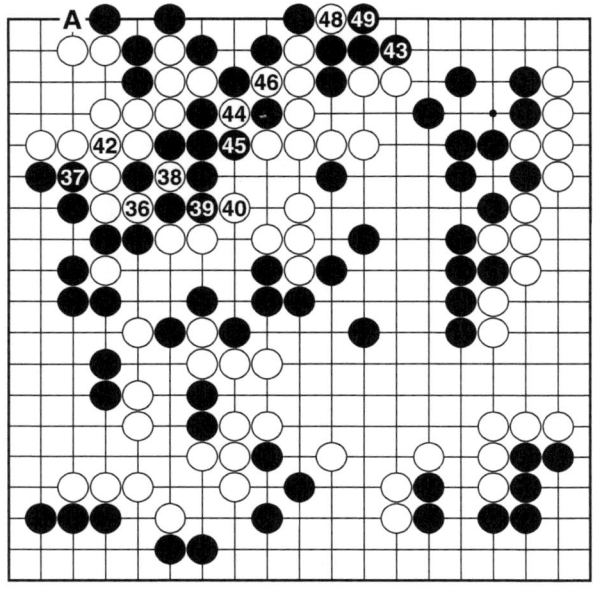

(136 – 149)

136 White cuts first and then reduces Black's liberties further with the following sequence and the throw-in at 144.

Black 141 takes ko
Black 147 connects at 144

149 If White plays at A, Black cannot connect everything anymore.

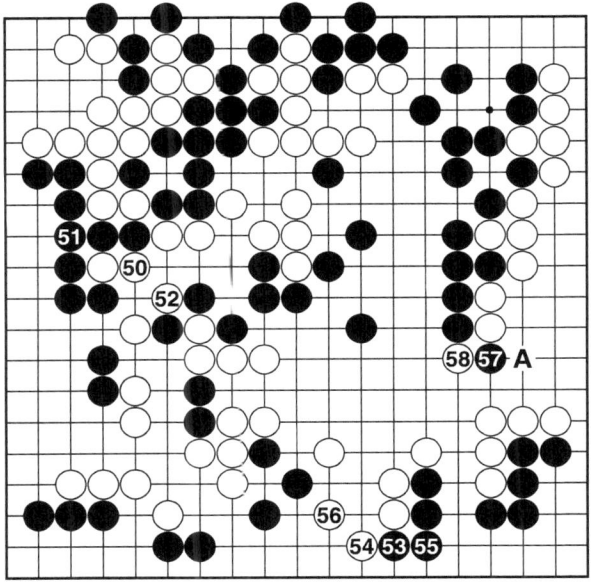

(150 – 158)

150 The mistake at 133 turned the game. At this point White is slightly ahead in the game. White seizes the opportunity, leading by about one point now.

157 A reducing move.

158 White should calmly answer the reducing move at A. But Park must have felt he needs to play a more powerful move. This turned out to be the losing move.

Park eventually expected the race in the variation where he would capture Black's stones, as his own stones in the center block the escape route. White must connect at 12, otherwise Black will cut and win the semeai.

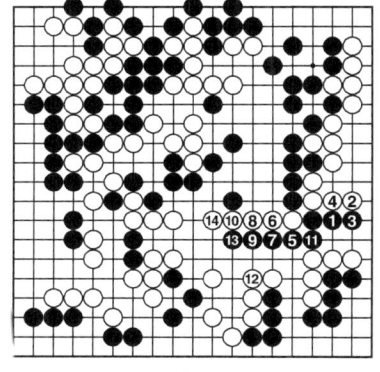

Variation

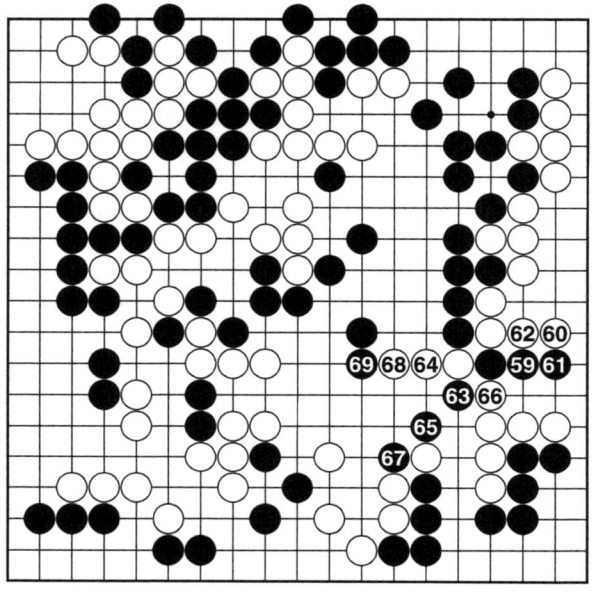

(159 – 169)

159 Shin was prepared to answer the cut. First, he plays the forcing moves on the right side before counterattacking with 163.

165 Tesuji! White cannot connect at 167 as Black would capture the two cutting stones with a move at 168.

166 White has to cut and capture the three of Black's stones. This doesn't hurt Black at all, as he has played these stones as kikashi and White is forced to play inside his own territory.

167 White's group at the bottom is now in danger.

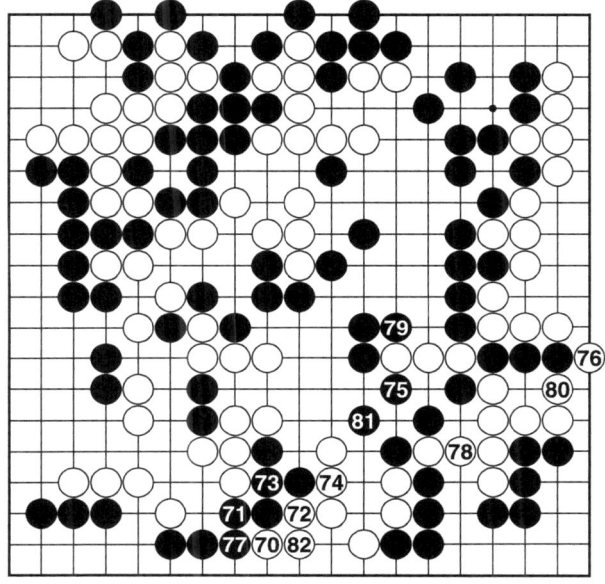

(*170 – 182*)

170 White plays sente moves at the bottom trying to make up for the loss. The game has once again been turned around.

180 White finally safely captures the stones on the right, but it is clearly visible that he did not gain anything from the cut at 158. On the contrary, the territory is even smaller now.

181 At this point Black is ahead by about one or two points.

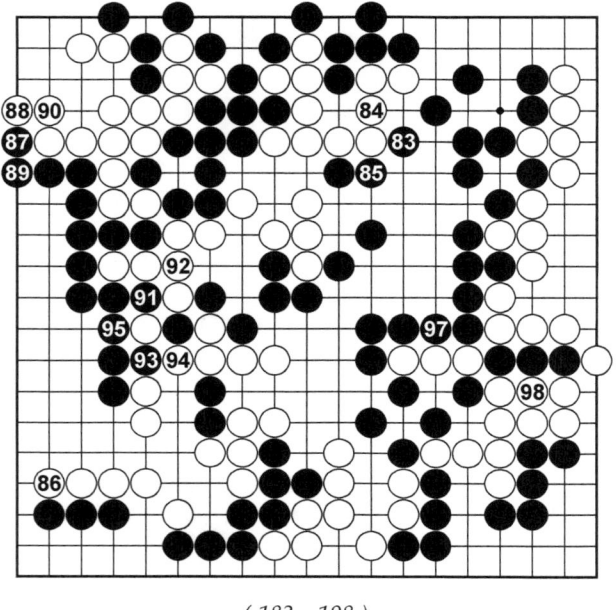

(183 – 198)

White 196 connects

183 A good move. White cannot afford to abandon these two stones.

187 At this stage Shin plays a series of sente moves until 204.

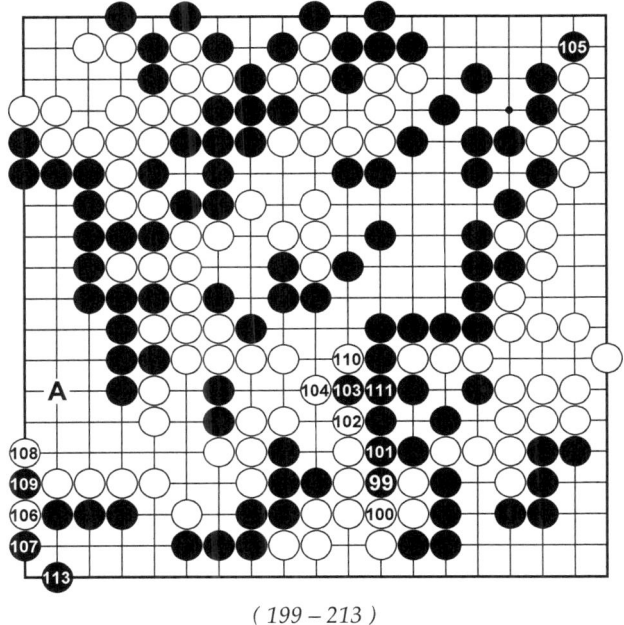

(199 – 213)

White 212 retakes the ko

205 This is a big endgame move, but A
on the left hand side would be even
bigger. Nevertheless Black is still leading by a small margin.

208 This is a good technique (a good move to remember) which will
allow White a wide slide into the upper area.

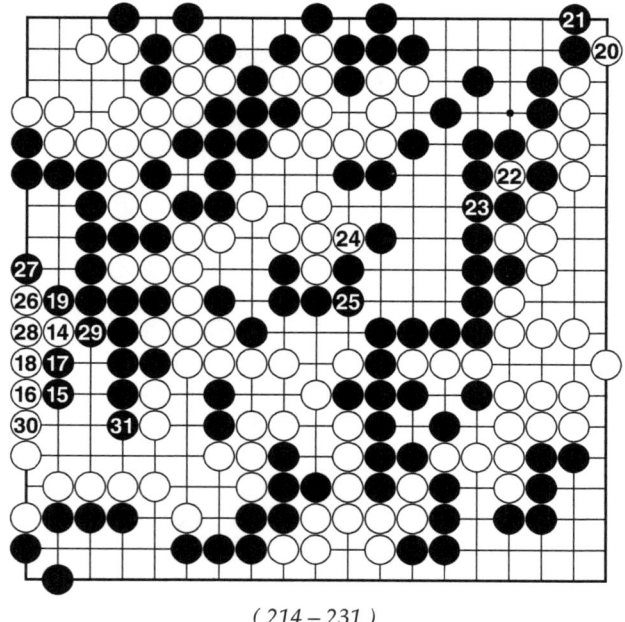

(214 – 231)

214 This jump was enabled by 208.

217 Black cannot cut off the stone at 214. The ko after 1 and 3 in the variation would be too risky for Black. His eye shape would require careful defense making him lose more points.

220 White is still behind, and Park is looking for a last chance.

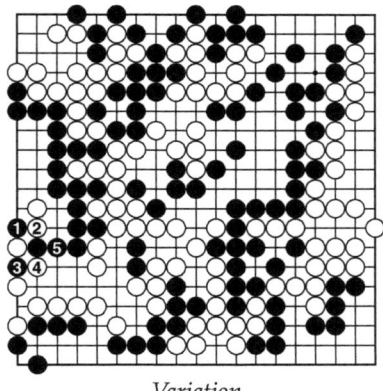

Variation

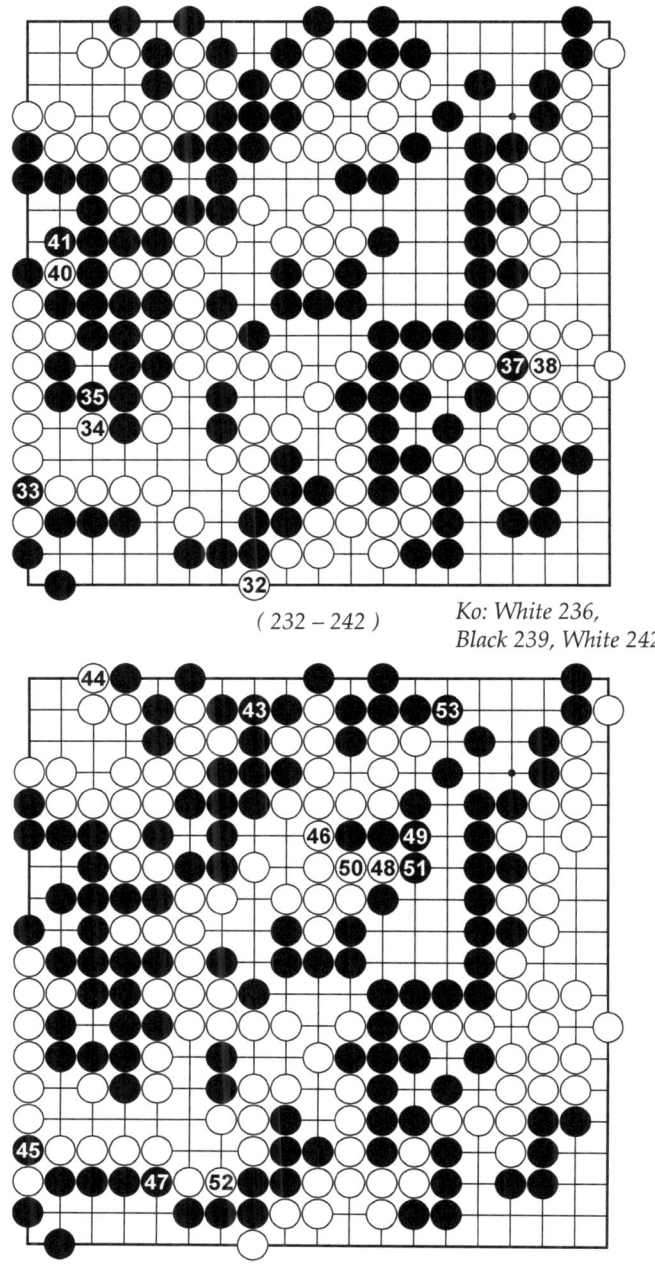

(232 – 242)

Ko: White 236,
Black 239, White 242

(243 – 253)

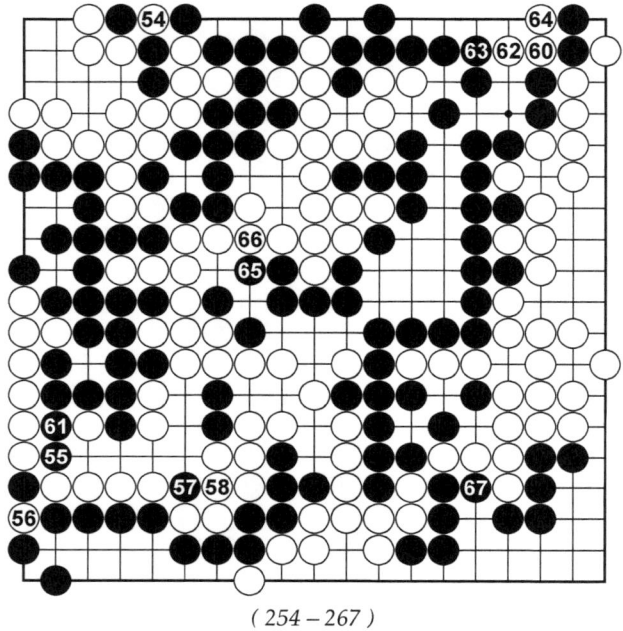

(254 – 267)

Black 259 at 233

255 White has had no time so far to defend
at 255, so Black starts the flower ko.

260 White doesn't have adequate ko threats.

261 Black accepts the trade and finishes the ko.

262 White takes the compensation.

267 After this move Park realizes there is no way to catch up
anymore. He finally resigns.

TWO

⚫ **Park Junghwan** ◯ **Shin Jinseo**

Date: 2020/10/21
Venue: Namhae German Village
Time: 90 min plus 5 × 1 min, Komi: 6.5

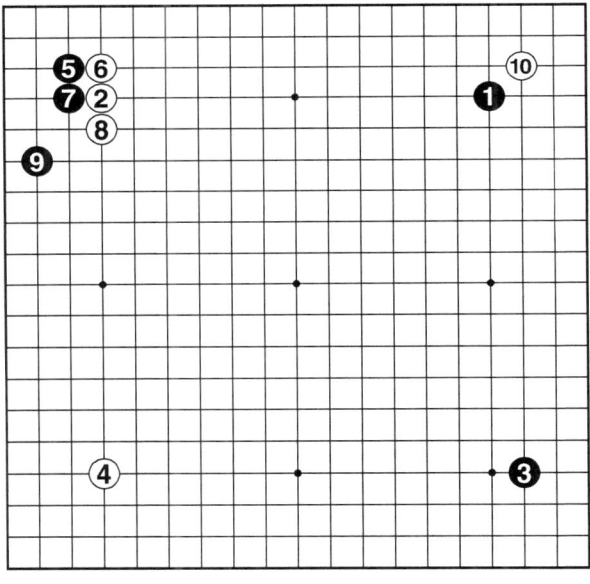

(1 – 10)

Namhae German Village is a very special place. Here live Korean people who went to Germany as miners and nurses and returned to Korea for their well deserved retirement. Since 2000, the new houses in the village were built in the traditional German style. Even the materials came from Germany! Beside the homes for families, guest houses were also established for tourists who want to enjoy this wondrous place.

8 Once again, White prefers a simple joseki variation to take sente for taking a big point.

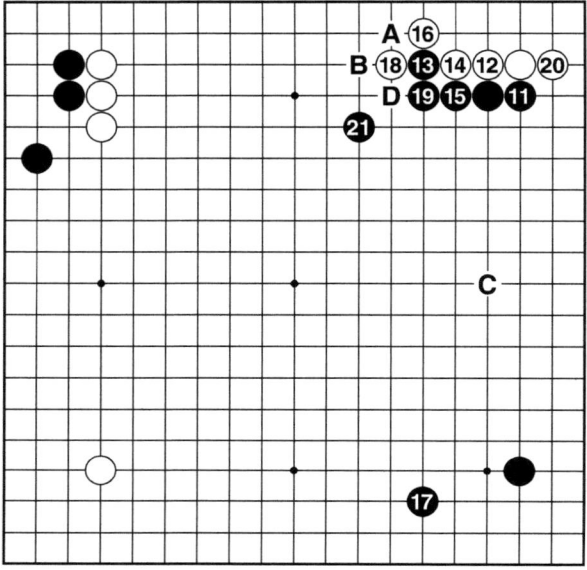

(11 – 21)

13 The keima is a move which became popular with AI, especially the follow up sequence starting at A. The complex and difficult variations arising from this attachement gave it the name Flying Dagger Joseki (see annex on page 135).

14 Black is not keen on going into this complex joseki and opts for a simple variation.

17 Up to now it's a normal modern opening. If Black extends at the top at 18, rather than at 17, White may exchange A for B and then take sente to approach the lower corner.

21 A move at C would also be a big point for Black. But the push at D and the following sequence in the variation would be very attractive for White, securing a nice area at the top.

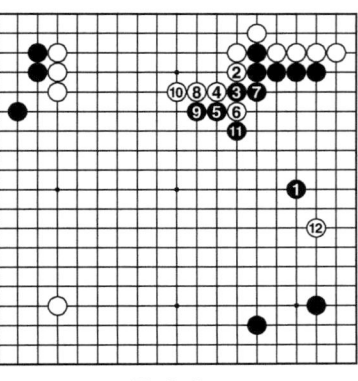

Variation

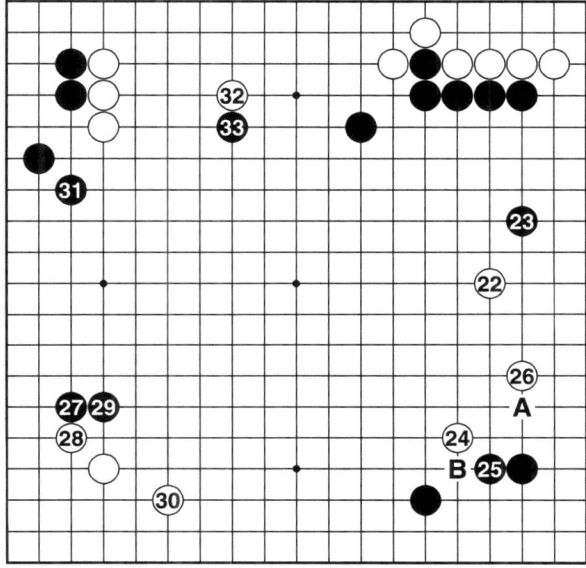

(22 – 33)

24 This move was appreciated by many observers. Usually such an approach move is played as a reduction at a later stage of a game. White 24 aims at developing the center. The more common approach would be at A, whereafter Black defends at B.

26 White creates a shape which is quite difficult to attack at the moment.

31 This is a very well balanced move for the right hand side. In case Black's choice would be a three space extension from 27 and 29, White would answer with pressing down at 31.

33 This is not only an AI style move, but it's exactly the move proposed by AI in this particular position. Park very likely thinks it's not worth to break up the upper side. The center is more important.

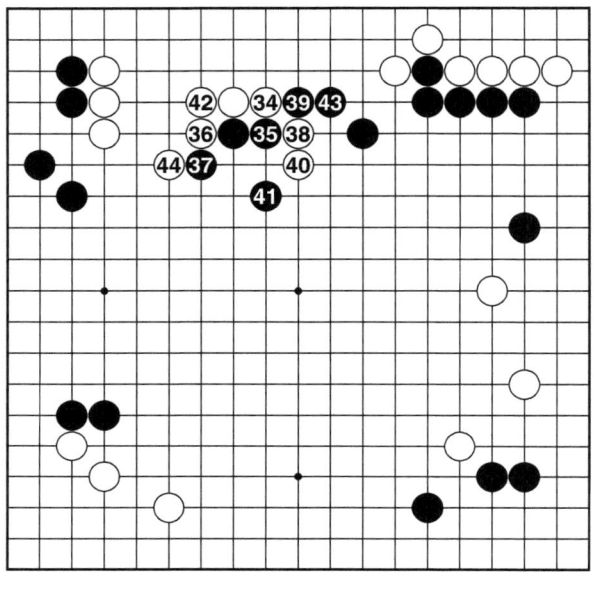

(34 – 44)

42 White needs to defend here. If White aims at capturing with 43, Black will fight back with the sequence shown in the variation. Black 10 is a splendid tesuji to break the upper side into pieces.

44 White intends to go out into the center and throw away the two stones at 38 and 40.

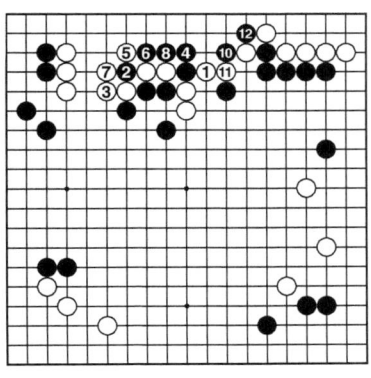

Variation

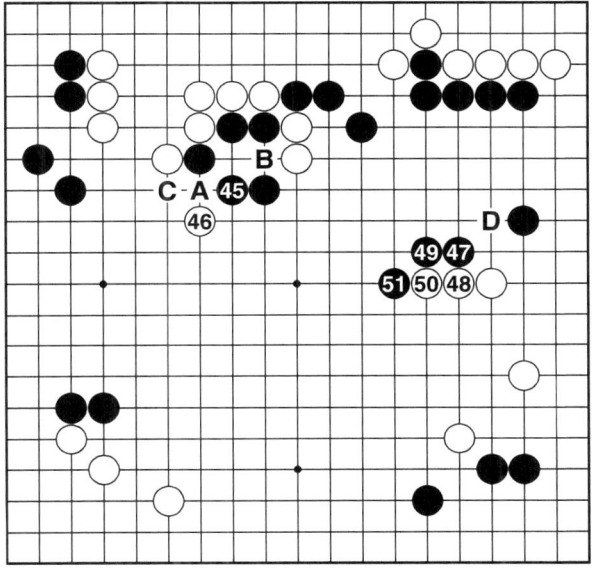

(45 – 51)

45 It's difficult for Black to make good shape here. If he extends to A, White will push like in the variation, forcing Black to extend even further while the aji of the two white stones at 38 and 40 would still not be eliminated.

AI recommends a trade: Black should play at 47. After the exchange of 48 and 49, White may come back to A, allowing Black to bend at 50. White still needs a move at B to capture.

46 This move is more active than just extending at C.

47 Safely capturing the two of White's stones is not good. White will attach at D to reduce the right hand side.

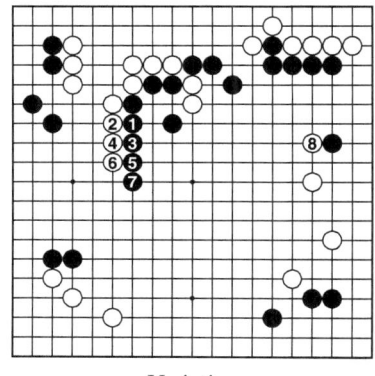

Variation

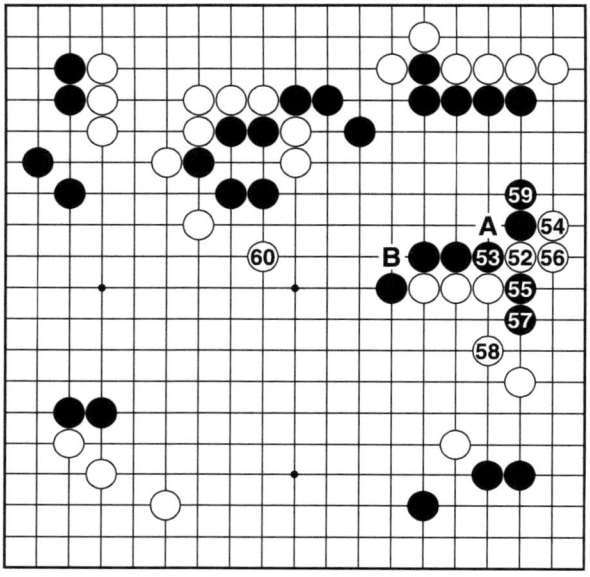

(52 – 60)

52 Attaching followed by the double hane at 54 is a strong combination, forcing Black to extend at 59.

55 Black doesn't want to cut at 56 and capture a stone at the edge as White would be able to counter with cuts at A and B. This result would be bad for Black. Before extending at 59, Park exchanges 55 and 57 to create trading possibilities for later.

58 To settle White's group at the right side, the variation in the diagram can be considered. This would be AI's first choice, but only by a very marginal difference. Shin may have been worried about allowing Black to jump to 4 in the center. That's why he chose 58, having already had in mind to ignore 59.

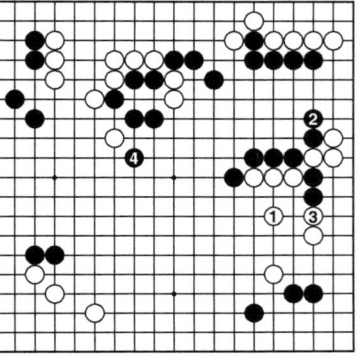

59 The move defends against a white atari here and threatens to capture three of White's stones.

60 White ignores 59 to play in the center first.

Variation

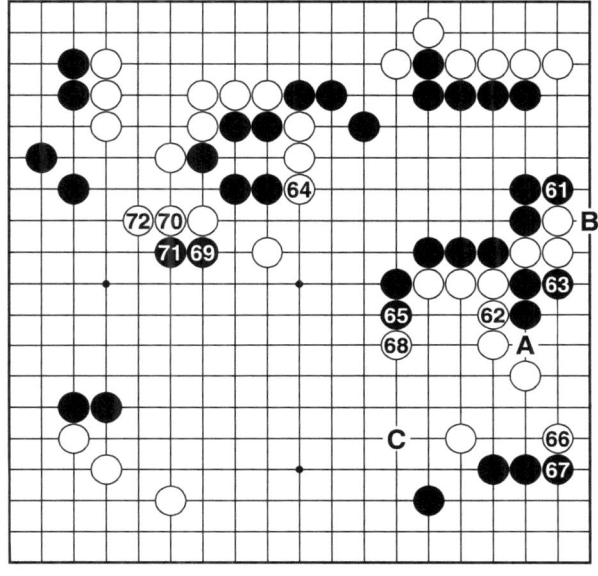

(61 – 72)

61 Park decides to trade his center stones against the three stones at the right side. White can thus play the forcing move at 62.

64 White finally takes the center. At this point the game is very balanced.

68 White has to do something about his group, which has no secure base yet. AI recommends to play the exchange A for B and then the jump to C.

69 Again, Park plays exactly the move proposed by AI. The idea is to sacrifice the center stones and develop the wide open area on the right side reaching into the center.

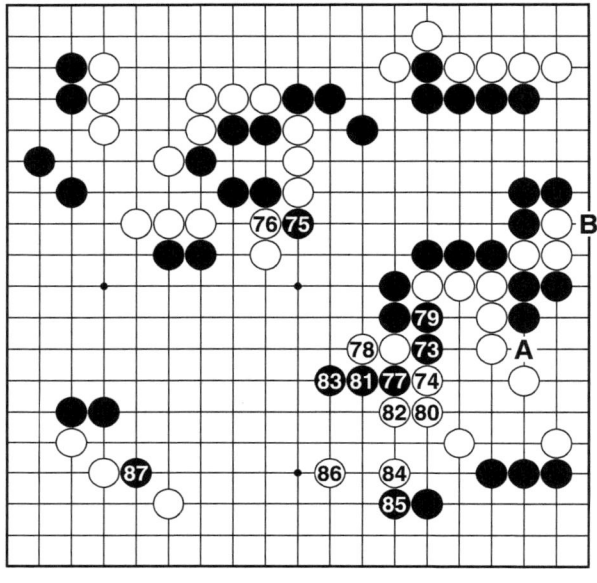

(73 – 87)

73 Beginning with Black 73, tactical fighting starts. It seems that
    Park was keen on punishing the dubious move at 68 somehow.
    He aims at putting pressure on White's group to gain more
    control of the center. However, AI rates the sequence up to 83 as
    a loss for Black, bringing the game back to a very well balanced
    state again.

84 A good technique to move out with the jump at 86. Playing the
    exchange of A for B first is still recommended by AI.

87 The bottom left corner now becomes the center of attention.

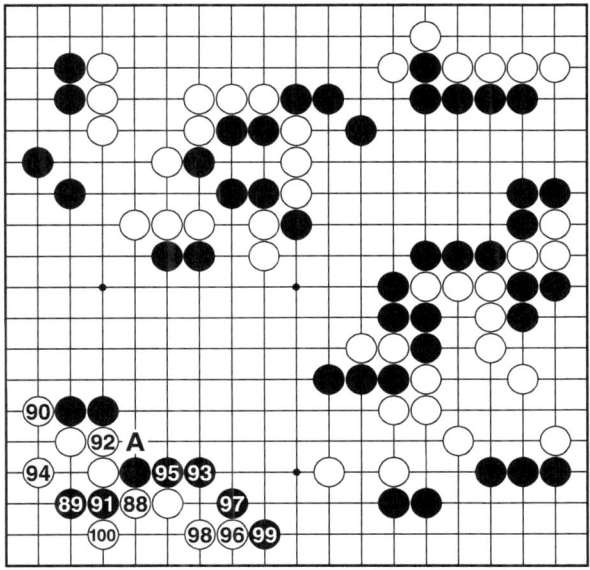

(*88 – 100*)

89 A strong move which White cannot simply answer by connecting at 91. A lot of variations emerge from this position.

90 Playing the hane first is not considered to be the best move as it leaves too much aji in the corner. Common practice locally, and AI recommendation, is to play the empty triangle at 92. If Black takes the opportunity to hane at the side it helps Black to settle the corner and remove the aji. After the variation in the diagram Black has sente to play either A or B.

91 The one and only move.

93 A very good move, aiming at sacrificing again to build strength and attack White's group on the right.

94 White cannot push at 95 as the capturing race in the corner is not good for him. The atari at A instead would lead to a tough fight where White has to care for three groups.

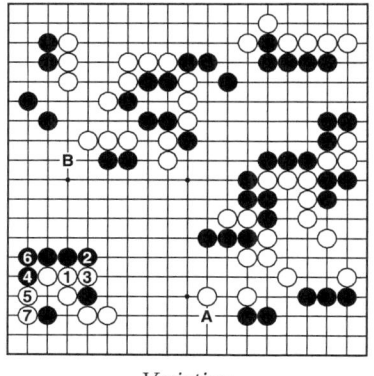

Variation

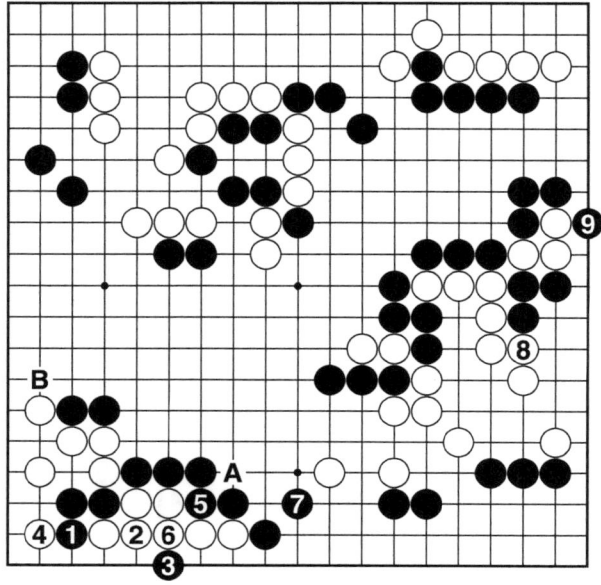

(101 – 109)

103 This move is not good as it removes the aji in the corner, the same for 105. Park may be worried that with a move at 105, White forces Black to connect at A, which would make a slight change in the endgame. AI does not regard this as important now. These moves were played too early.

107 Black should have played simply here. Without 103 to 106, White must be worried about a block at B. This concern is gone now.

Another variation considered playable for Black is shown in the diagram. Black cuts first on the right to force White to make life by capturing three stones. Then Black covers the cut at 5, taking profit. The result would be a very close game.

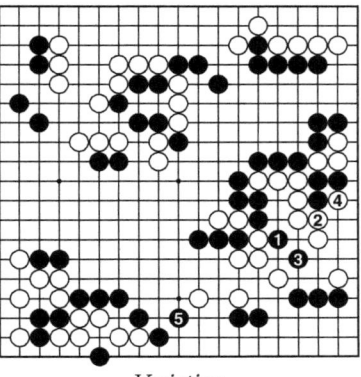

108 A necessary defense move to forestall Black 1 and 3 in the variation. At this point the game is very close.

Variation

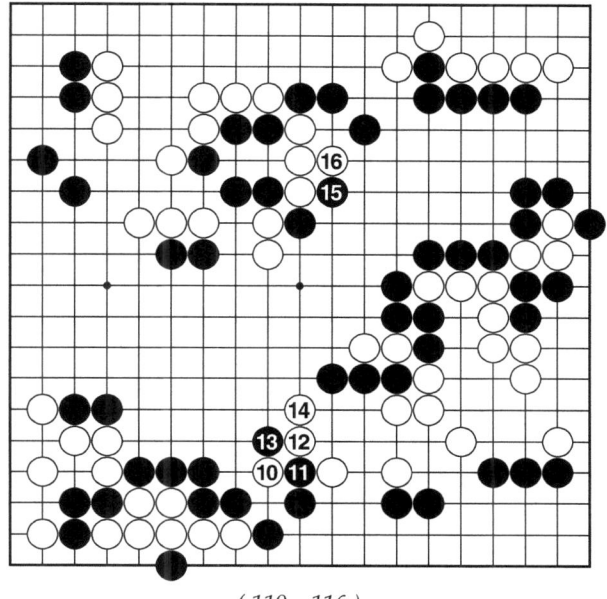

(110 – 116)

110 This move shall take control of the center. However, it's a mistake. White should play the forcing sequence 1 to 6 in the variation and then jump to 7. This would keep the close game going.

115 At this stage Black has a small lead of about one point and a half.

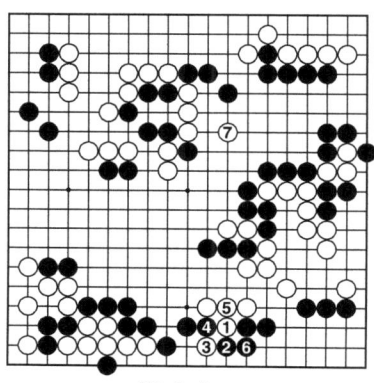

Variation

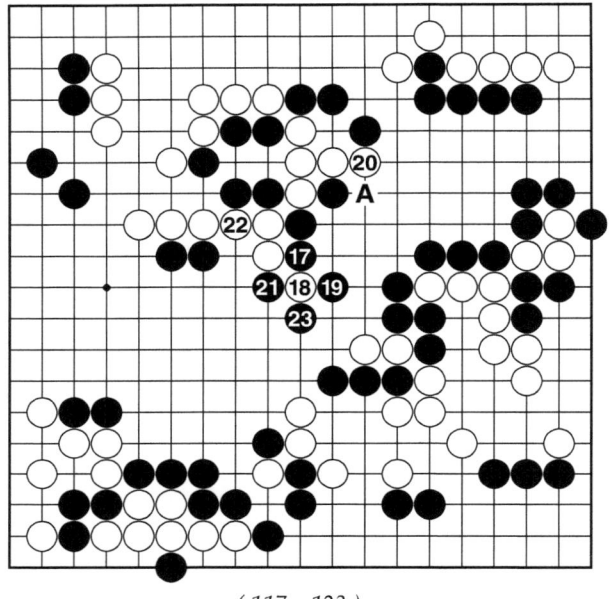

(117 – 123)

117 This move is a mistake on Black's part. Instead, he should simply extend at A to block the territory at the top. The appropriate sequence is shown in the diagram, providing Black with a good result.

119 Again, Black misses the chance to defend at A and prevent White from breaking in.

120 White now seizes the opportunity to break into Black's area. Black's mistake turned the game into a small lead for White.

121 Black cannot cut at 122 and so he trades again. But the ponnuki in the center doesn't gain him much.

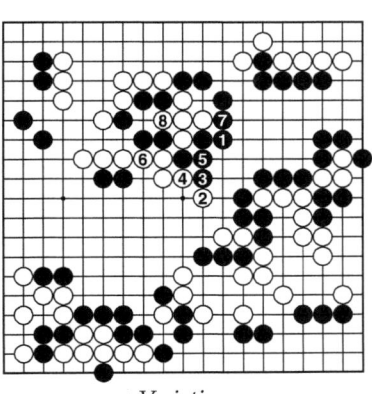

Variation

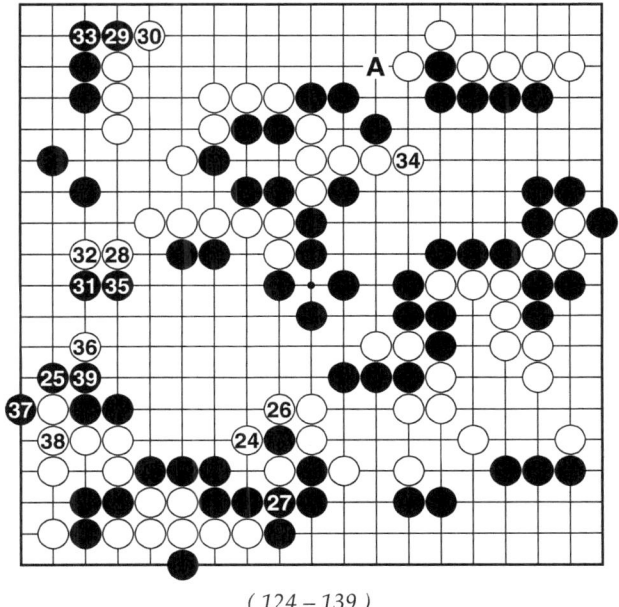

(*124 – 139*)

124 A big move. Counting is not easy in this situation, even for top professional players. It will be a tough endgame.

128 Big points would also be A or the cut at 139, both playable before the kosumi at 128.

134 Bending at 135 is bigger according to AI analysis.

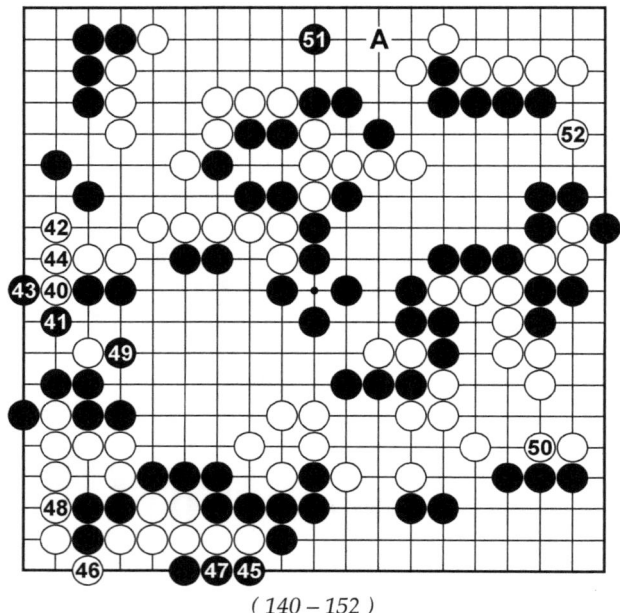

(140 – 152)

150 AI prefers the defense at A. The game is still very close.

152 Again, AI analysis calculates A as the move to keep the game close. After 134, Black's area is already open from the other side. After White 152, the game is slightly in favor of Black, by about one and half to two points. This shows how close the game is and how it hinges on the edge.

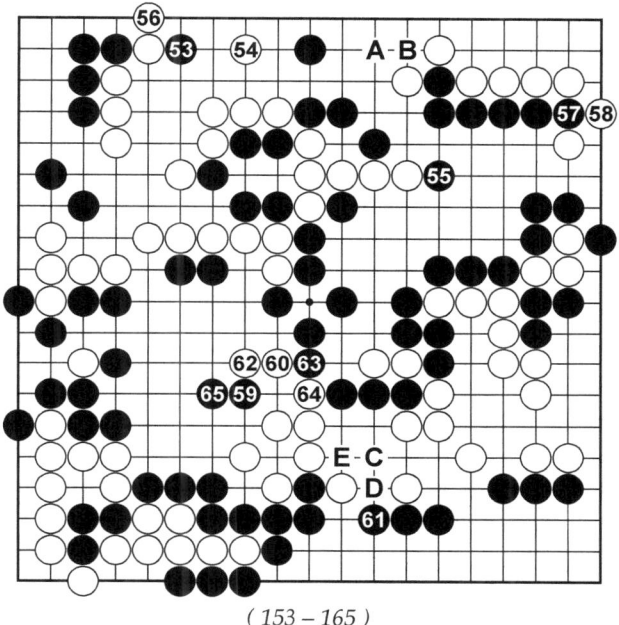

(153 – 165)

153 Black's plan expects a direct answer by White, allowing him to play 154 himself. This would be good for Black, even if White extends to edge with 154. However, it would have been better to exchange A for B first and then jump to 154.

154 White doesn't follow Black's plan. Has this response gotten Park off track and caused a psychological impact? Does he feel he has fallen behind?

155 As the variation shows, Black cannot capture the white stone at the top.

164 This move is necessary to avoid being cut off by the sequence Black C to E.

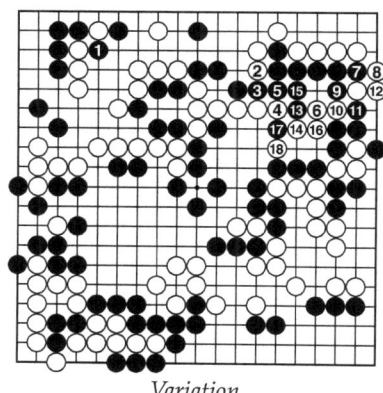

Variation

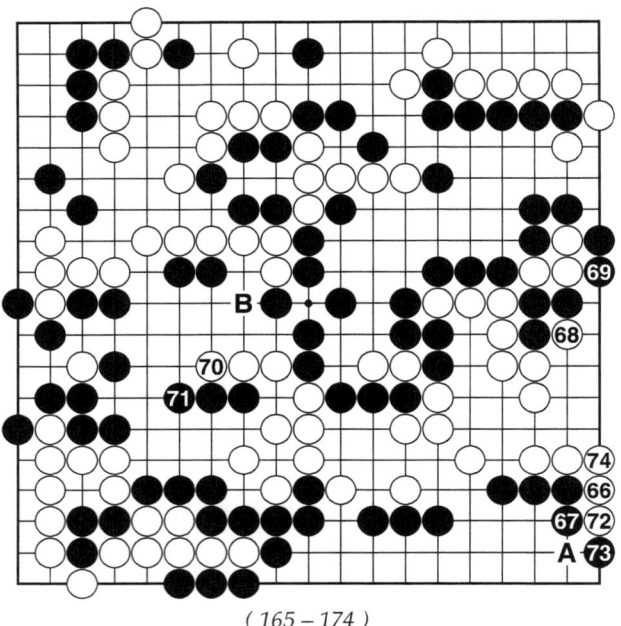

(165 – 174)

166 The game is very close.

167 This move can hardly be explained. Even top players fail to find a potential reasoning behind this move. Any amateur would block here properly at A.
The question remains: Was this an unlucky accident?

172 White continues to push into the corner. When Black defends now with 173 and A, he has lost two points here compared to blocking with 167 at 172.
However, the endgame is still difficult. AI recommends for White to play at A first to eliminate the ko aji.

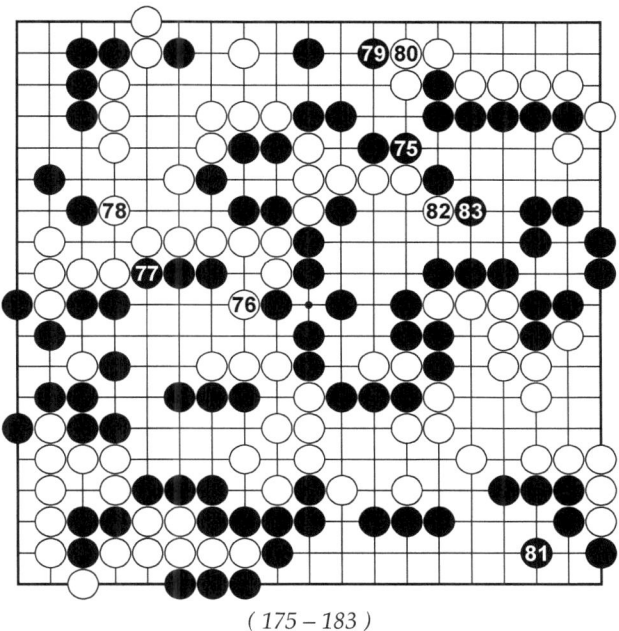

(175 – 183)

175 It's not clear whether Black can win the ko in the variation or gain something from fighting the ko. However, this might give a better chance of winning than connecting with the move actually played in the game.

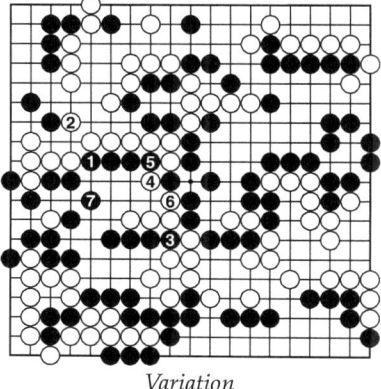

Variation

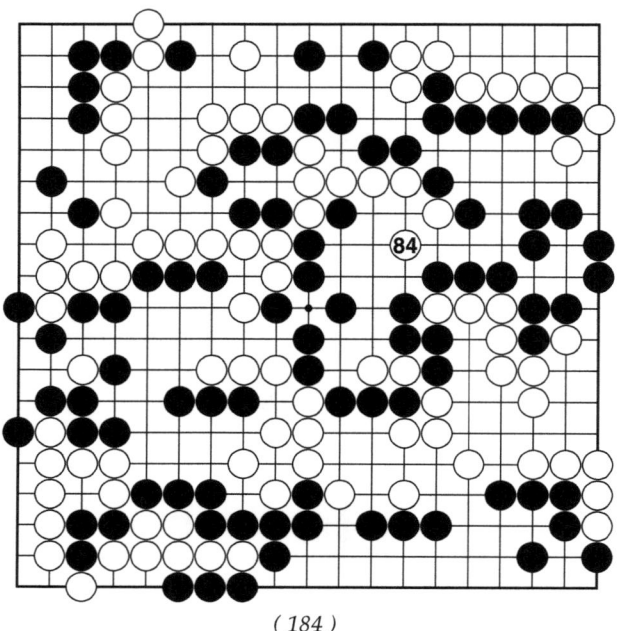

(184)

184 The game is still quite close. White leads by about a point and
a half. Eventually Park considers the loss of the area supposed
to be surrounded by his top right group too big. He resigns at
this point.
There were voices which said resigning at this point was too
early.

THREE

● **Shin Jinseo**   ○ **Park Junghwan**

Date: 2020/10/22
Venue: Sangju Eun Sand Beach
Time: 90 min plus 5 × 1 min, Komi: 6.5

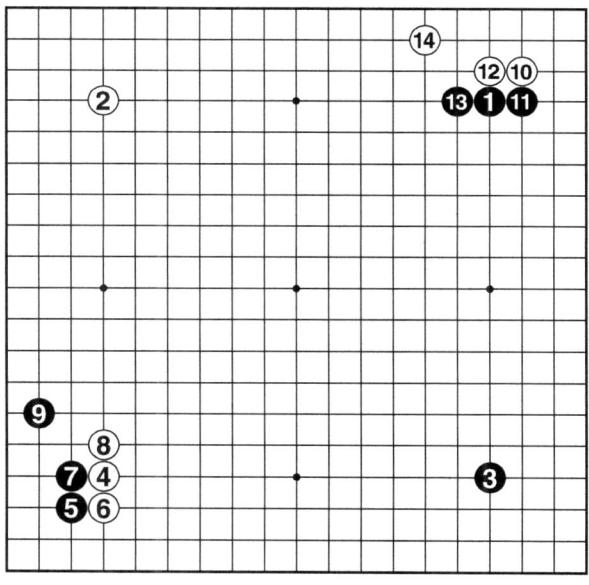

(1 – 14)

Sangju Silver Sand Beach is a popular tourist attraction. Many people come here to enjoy the sand, water, and groves. The wide shores with shallow waters stretch out for about two kilometers and are perfect for families and people looking to relax.

The summer temperatures did not linger for Park and Shin, so their outdoor game had to be played under heaters. Shin said after the game: „The sound of the waves during the middle game was fine, this allowed me to focus on Baduk."

14   The same very simple modern joseki is played here, twice even. Are these prospects of a peaceful game or are the players setting the scene for some heavy fighting?

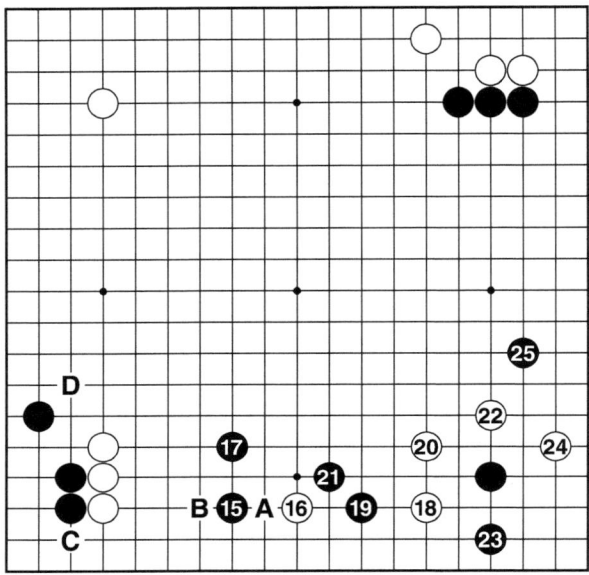

(15 – 25)

15   This is a normal approach to the three stone wall. If you choose to play A instead, White can easily make a base with B. In this position AI prefers to simply play a shimari at 18.

16   White doesn't like to settle the corner starting with the hane at C. The counter pincer is a good alternative.

21   After White 20, Black is spoiled for choices. Defending the corner with a shimari is an option. In the game, Black covers White's single stone to settle his group and forestall a white kosumi at the same point. AI's choice is a tenuki at D.

23   The variation shows the AI's proposal, but Shin may have feared that White 6 is putting too much pressure on Black's three stones above. So Black just lives in the corner without making White strong.

25   Blocking the corner now is too passive for Black. He plays on the outside to force an answer by White.

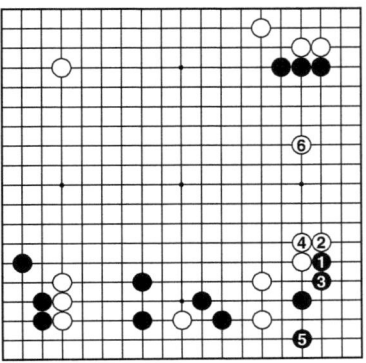

Variation

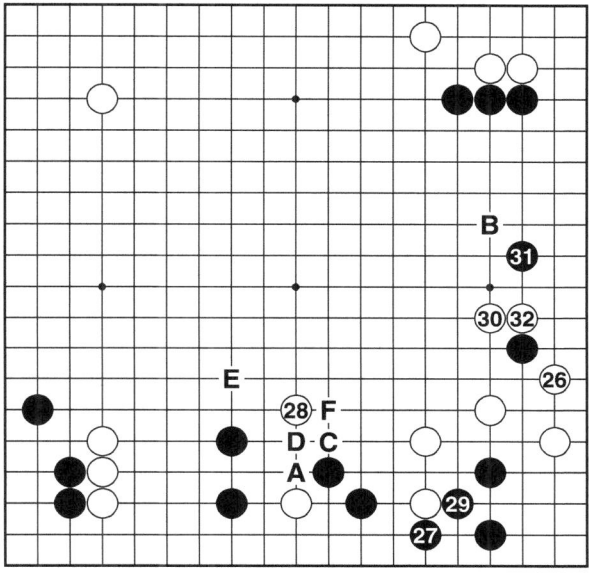

(26 – 32)

26 If White jumps into the corner now, Black is happy to fight with the variation in the diagram.

28 An interesting move. If Black answers at A, White has sente to play 29 and then attack at B. But Shin decides to ignore this move and to reinforce his group at 29.

30 AI recommends to start moving at A in order to separate Black's groups. The follow up of Black C to White F is one way of playing. Very likely, a battle with several running groups would evolve. Note that without the exchange of Black 25 for 26, White could have played the wider extension at B.

31 Crawling at 32 is not good for Black. The single stone served its purpose already. In addition, if Black crawls out White will build a strong wall facing the center.

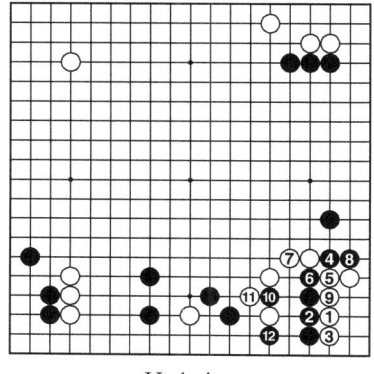

Variation

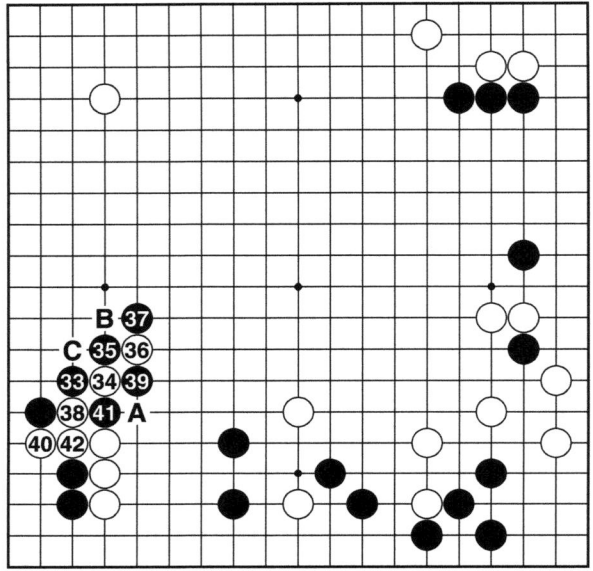

(33 – 42)

36 The usual order here is 38 first and then 36, which is also prefered by AI. However, there is an increasing number of games where White actually plays the hane at 36 first.

37 Black could simply atari at 41. White must answer at 39 and Black can push through at A. This would be a good result for Black, giving him a small advantage. But Shin played the astonishing triple hane at 37, a pretty fancy move nowadays. Extending at B would also have been an option.

38 Black has two ways to answer. Both connecting at C and the cut in the game are playable.

39 Shin played this cut already earlier this year in the final of the Korean league.

41 The variation is considered slightly better for Black, as there remains more aji in the corner after 3 and 5.

42 The result after the trade is well balanced.

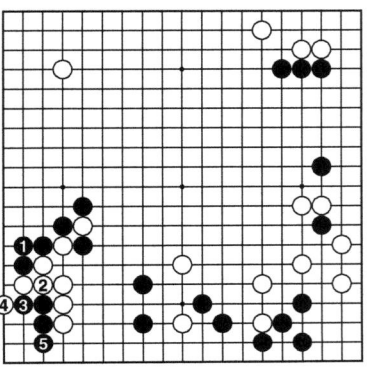

Variation

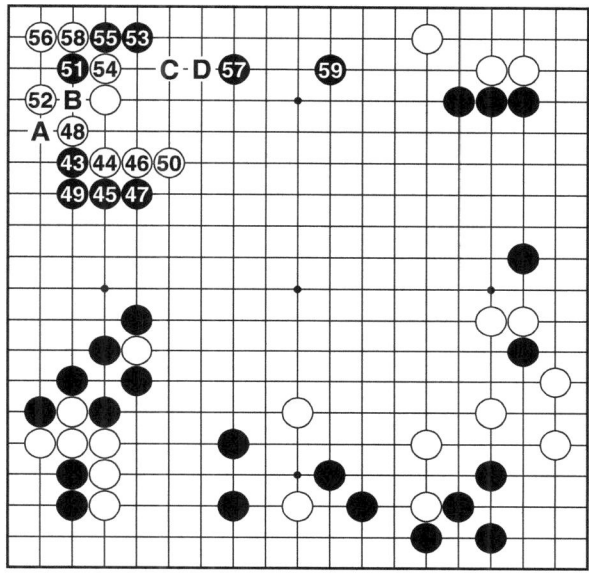

(43 – 59)

47   The push at 47 is another surprise in this game. This move made an early of its rare appearances in 1975, played by Miyamoto Yoshihisa 9p against Fujisawa Hosai 9p. Common sense is that White cannot be allowed the good move at 48. AI prefers the kosumi at A. But B and 51 are also playable, even the actual move is not completely out of question.

50   This move might be better placed at C or D to protect the corner.

51   Black invades the corner to build a base at the top.

52   White cannot allow Black to connect so easily to erase the corner.

54   The variation shows another option for White. It's painful for Black to live in the corner, but Park didn't like giving it away.

59   At this point the game is slightly better for Black.

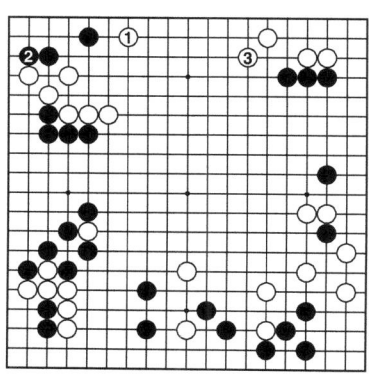

Variation

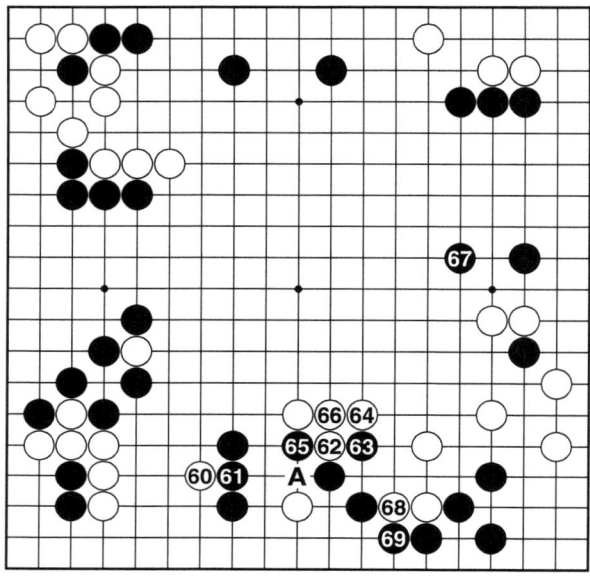

(60 – 69)

62 White would like to take influence in the center.

63 Black doesn't want to give White sente so easily. Black 63 and 65 allow him to play the big point at 67. AI considers defending at A suffcient, as White's shape remains thin and Black may make use of a kikashi from the upper side. The difference, however, is marginal.

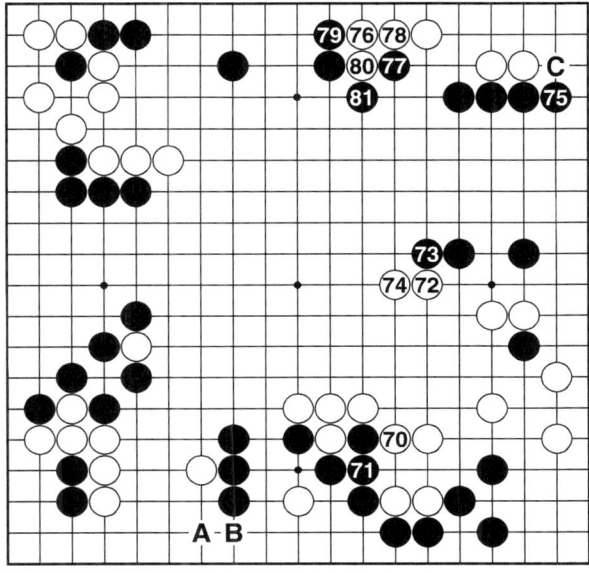

(70 – 81)

72 White should first exchange A for B at the bottom.

73 AI considers a move at A, preventing a white forcing move here, to be a bit bigger for Black.

75 A big move. This may not be sente against the life of the corner, but a lot of territory is at stake there. Black has built a small lead of about one and a half points so far.

76 Blocking at C is a rather passive way to answer Black 75. Therefore, White jumps on the second line to enlarge his corner first.

77 Blocking at 79 is not good as it would drive White out into the center. So Black peeps first to limit White's room to maneuver.

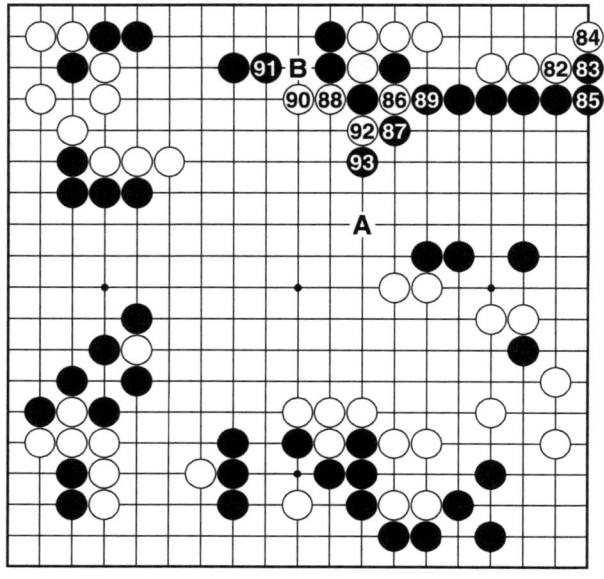

(82 – 93)

83 This move looks very early but it's extremely big. As it prevents a sente engame by White, it should indeed be played as soon as possible.

86 Defending the corner is too slow. White cannot allow Black to play A, this would make it to easy for him.

91 This looks like the shape move, but AI actually recommends playing the empty triangle at B here. It considers 91 to be a one point loss.

93 This is a mistake. Black should simply connect like in the variation. White has to defend the corner and Black can take the initiative to secure his lead of roughly two points. But Shin did not care and went for the first fight.

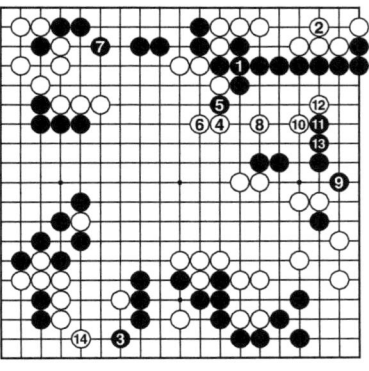

Variation

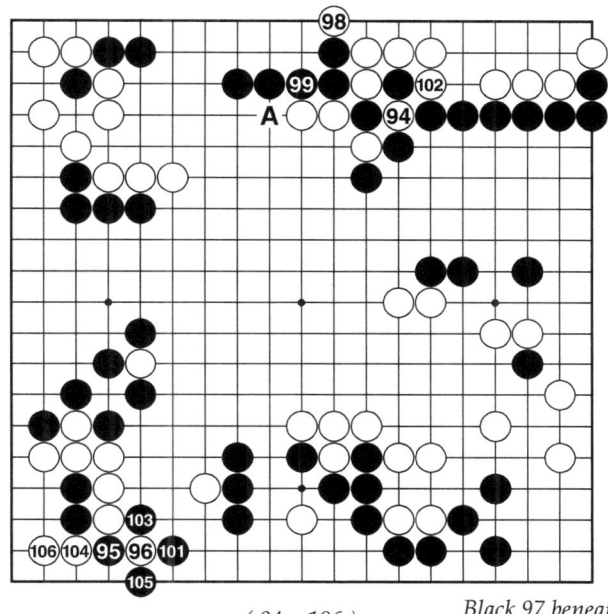

(94 – 106)

Black 97 beneath 94;
White 100 below 94;

95 Black makes use of the aji in the lower left to fight the ko.

99 If Black had played 91 at 99 he could now answer 98 with A, taking another liberty from White's stones.

102 Finishing the ko is a mistake. Park misses a good chance to make the game complicated. The fight in the diagram is a difficult one but White can win the ko and keep the game close.

106 After the ko has been decided, the result is good for Black. The ponnuki at the bottom is big. In the center it's very hard to make points for either side. White's mistake allowed Black to take the lead again. Black is ahead by about two points.

Ko:
Beneath 2: White 5, 11, 17
At 2: Black 8, 14

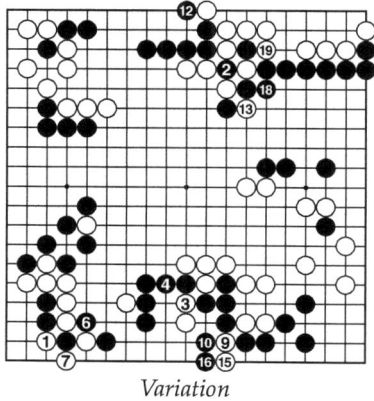

Variation

55

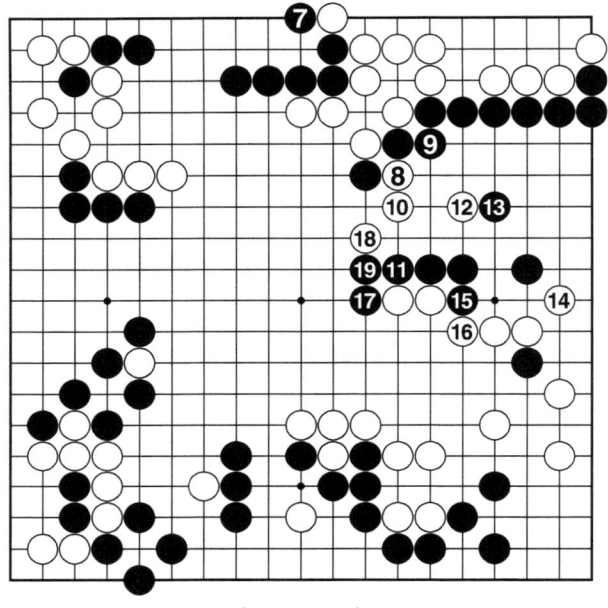

(107 – 119)

107 Black has no time to defend against White 108, the group at the top must not die.

111 This move is a bit slack. AI recommends defending the territory here with the sequence in the variation.

112 Now White can jump into Black's area.

114 As White damaged Black's territory already, this kosumi is a mistake. White should play either 122 or the hane at 119 instead. At this stage AI considers controlling the center more valuable.

117 Black comes first to play the hane in the center.

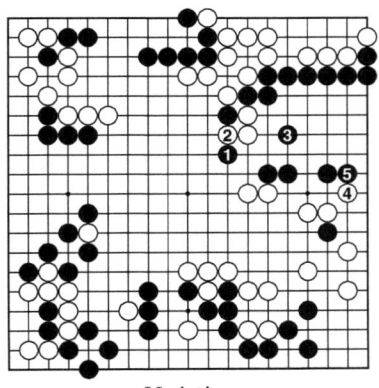

Variation

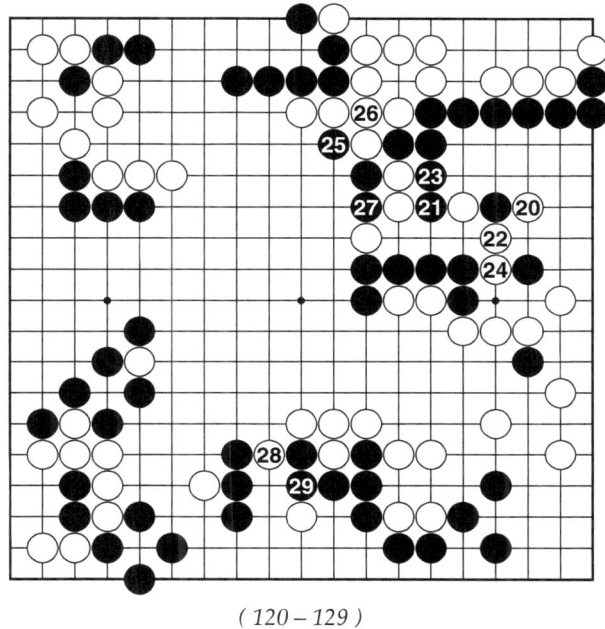

(*120 – 129*)

121 A nice tesuji. Black trades its former territory against the center.

129 Black's lead has increased to about three points.

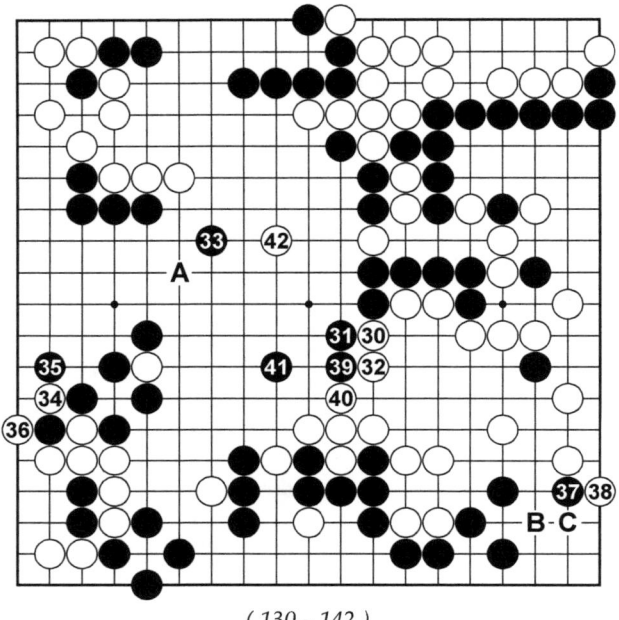

(130 – 142)

130 This is almost the last chance for White now. Therefore, he should try a more aggressive approach like A to reduce the center. White 130 is too slow.

133 The center turns pretty black now.

134 This move is gote for White. Instead he should play the big move at B.

137 A big move. Shin pretends to take the corner, but...

139 ...changes direction with the push at 139. Simply blocking at C and following the regular endgame would be sufficent. This would solidify the lead of about five points.

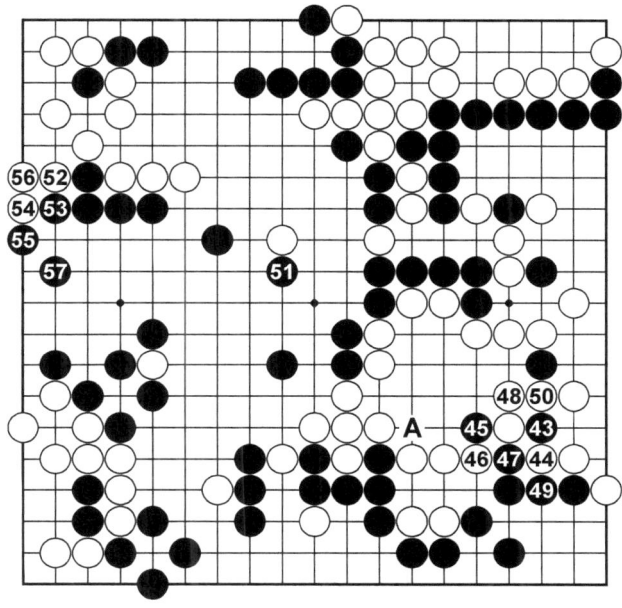

(*143 – 157*)

143 A nice endgame sente sequence, which also forces White to defend at A later on. However, AI analysis considers this sequence to be a loss of about one point.

150 White should exchange first 1 to 4 in the variation, reducing the corner before defending at 5.

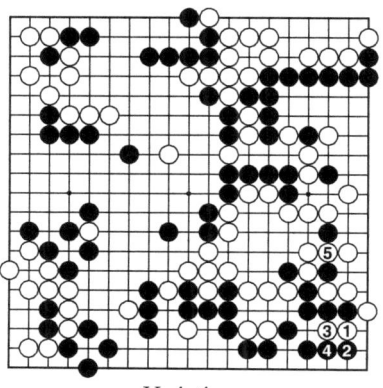

Variation

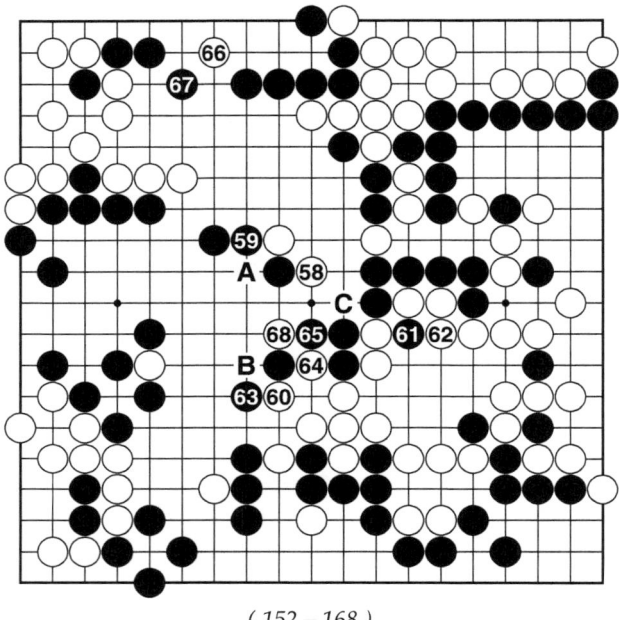

(*152 – 168*)

159 Simply extending at A would be more than enough, but Shin wants to take as many points as possible.

160 This is White's last attempt to complicate things, but maybe it's too late already.

161 This is good timing. Later White might not want to answer here anymore.

163 Again, Black is not in favour of a calm response like extending at B.

166 This is a preparation move to create ko threats before actually starting the ko in the center.

168 Black cannot avoid the ko by defending at B. White would keep the ko alive with C.

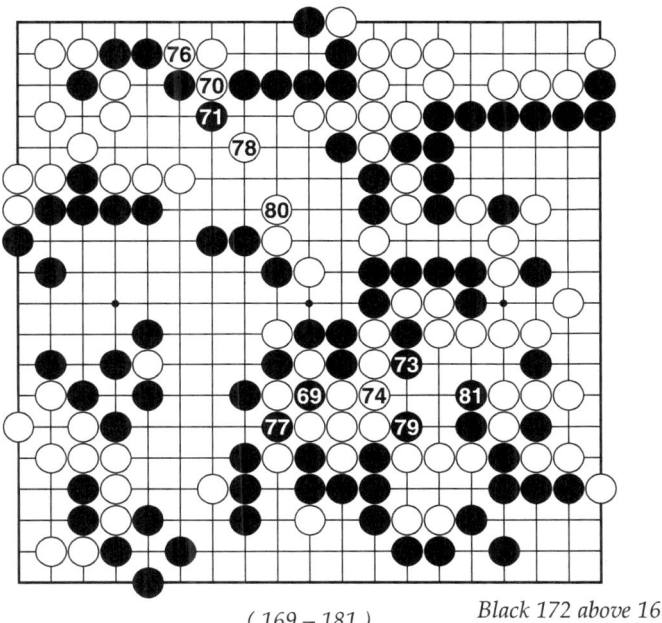

(169 – 181)

Black 172 above 169;
White 175 at 169

174 Ignoring the atari of 173 to win the ko is not a successful path for White, as the variation shows. White's gain equals the loss.

177 Black sacrifices his top group to finish the ko.

178 White needs another move to complete the trade and capture Black's group.

179 Black's capture is increased by another eight stones in the center.

181 And Black captures the bamboo joint as well.

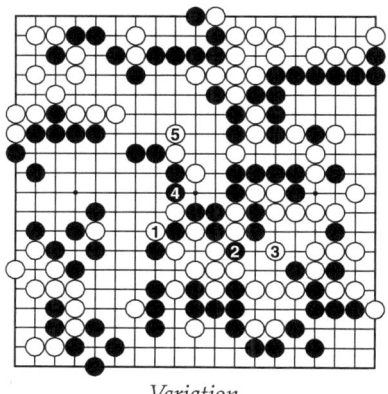

Variation

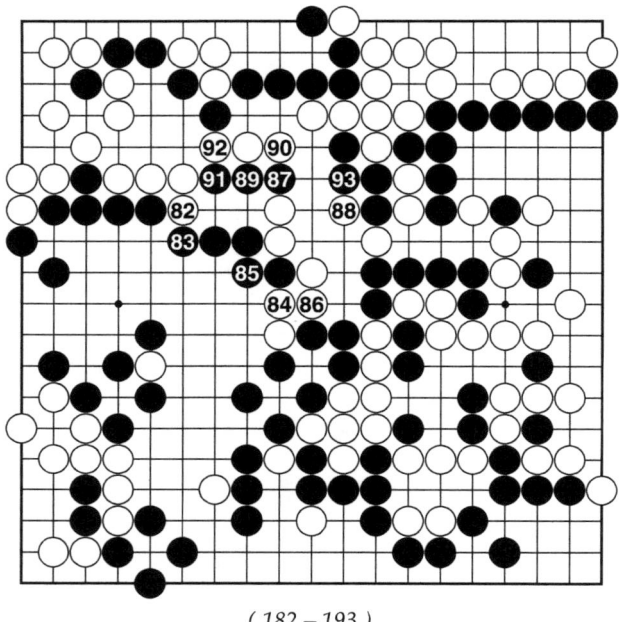

(182 – 193)

186 This move doesn't really work, but White cannot afford giving up these stones.

187 A nice tesuji, threatening either to capture White's stones in the center or to revive Black's group at the top.

193 After this move White resigns. He would have either lost more stones in the center or had to face another ko (see the variation). Black has big ko threats, for instance to make his group at the top alive again.

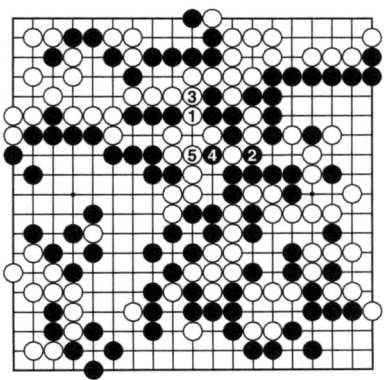

Variation

FOUR

● **Park Junghwan** ○ **Shin Jinseo**

Date: 2020/11/11
Venue: Namhae-gak Motel
Time: 90 min plus 5 × 1 min, Komi: 6.5

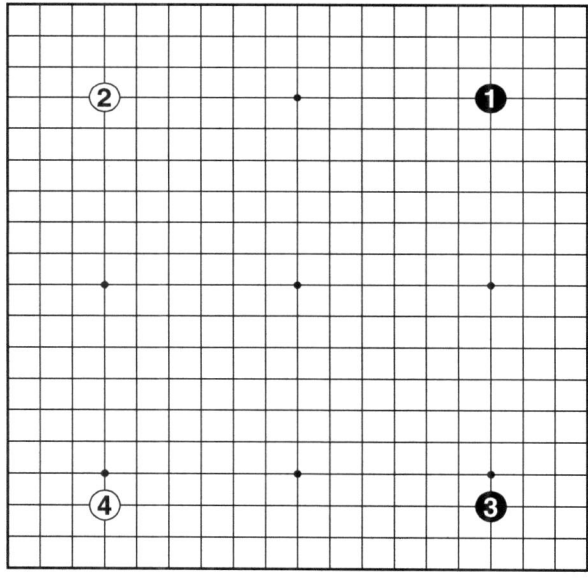

(1 – 4)

On June 22, 1973, the Namhae Bridge, the first suspension bridge in Korea, was opened. The Namhae Island was thereby connected to the main land, promoting social and economic development. The Namhae Bridge itself became a popular tourist attraction and in 1975 the Namhae-gak Motel was opened at the bridge's entrance.

Shin is leading this seven game match 3:0. The national trainer Hong Min-pyo 4p said that it was expected that Shin will dominate the series, but starting off with a clear 3:0 lead was a big surprise. The national trainer Mok Jin-seok 9p explained that Park was following a strategy to play calmly in the first three games and wait for a chance to take the lead in the endgames. In a balanced game, this is a reasonable plan offering plenty of opportunities for Park.

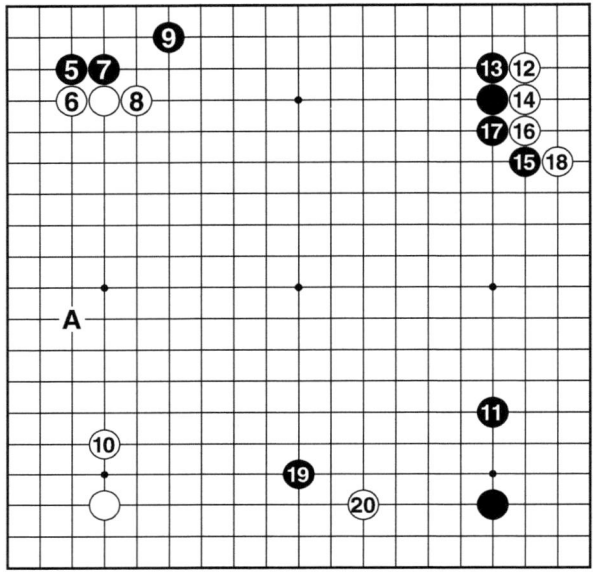

(5 – 20)

8   In the upper left corner, Shin again chooses a simple joseki. It seems like the favorite joseki of the two players in this match. It has been used in each and every of their games so far, by both of them.

15   Once more, Park plays the invitation to enter the famous Flying Dagger Joseki, but Shin refuses with 16.

20   This is a very active invasion. A more peaceful continuation would be a move on the left side, e.g. at A. The variation shows another way seen in professional games. After White 3, Black has sente to attach the shimari with 4. Shin may not have liked Black to build such a vast sphere of influence so early in the game. White's aim is to break this ambition with 20.

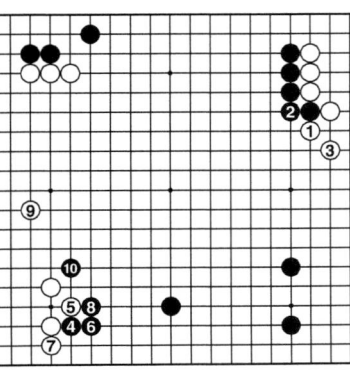

Variation

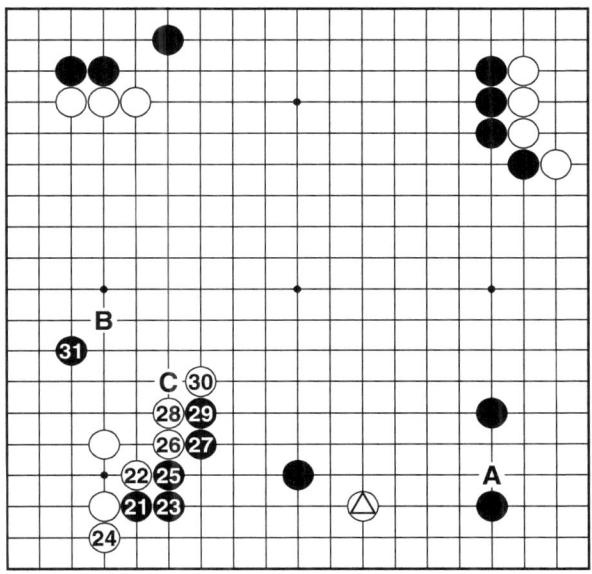

(21 – 31)

21 Park ignores the invasion and attaches at the shimari in the lower left corner anyway. This move is pretty much sente for Black.

26 Locally this move is joseki. From a global point of view the attachment at A looks reasonable now. But also an extension around B can be considered here.

30 With the wall at the top and the marked white stone already in place, extending at C is clearly not an option here.

31 The cut at C, as shown in the variation, was the expected move. If White doesn't want to push from behind he can simply play 4 at A. Instead of 3, Black cannot really extend at B in the variation because the marked white stone makes his own group rather thin.

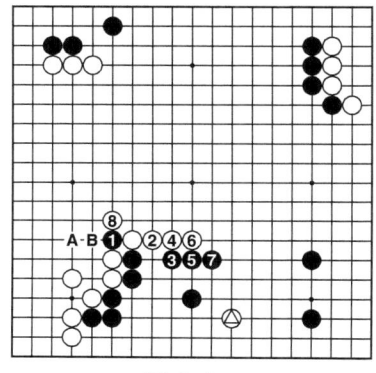

Variation

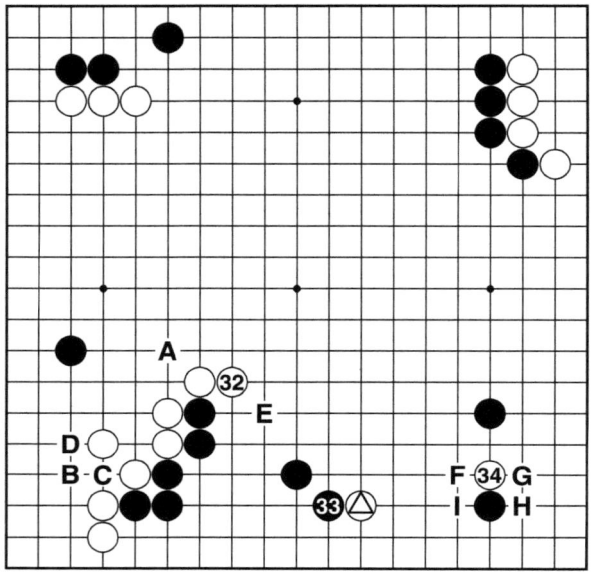

(32 – 34)

32 Defending against the cut with A is a slow move. Shin would never play such a slow move. Black would peep at B and then extend at D erasing the left side. Shin wants to make use of the marked stone. That's why he extends at 32.

33 This is a counter attack. A simple defense at E is recommended by AI, but Park prefers to attack and build a base.

34 White plays a probe first to see how Black responds. Black has four choices: from F to I. The variation shows a reasonable sequence. As the ladder is good for White, Black must connect at 7 and White can extend to 8.

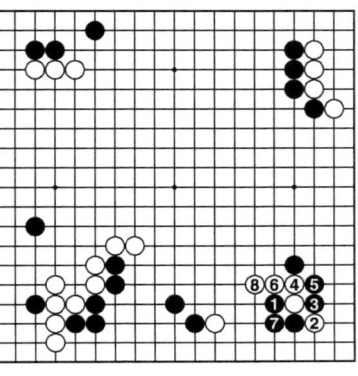

Variation

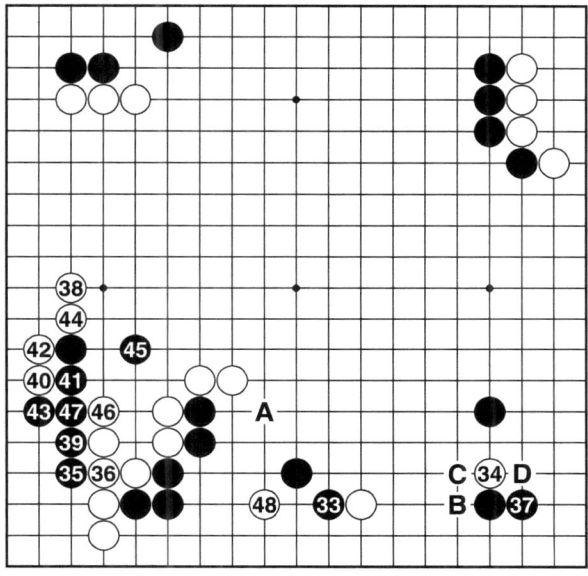

(35 – 48)

35 Before answering the probe, Black plays the kikashi at 35.

37 The ladder is good for White so Black cannot choose the variation on page 66. Therefore Black draws back to avoid a fight starting from this corner.

38 White leaves the two stones alone to attack Black's stone on the left side. White 40 strikes at the vital point.

48 After the left side has been settled Shin takes a long time to think about his next move. It was expected that White would exchange 1 for 2 as in the variation and then play 3 to enclose Black. If Black plays 4 at 5, White would get perfect shape with 4. That's why Black peeps at 4, but White counters with 5. If Black cuts now at 7 then White A would kill Black. So Black must secure life with 6 and 8. In the game, Shin decides to invade at 48, starting a difficult fight.

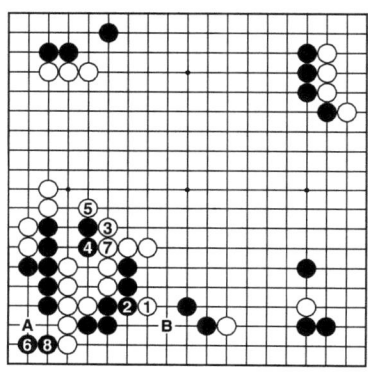

Variation

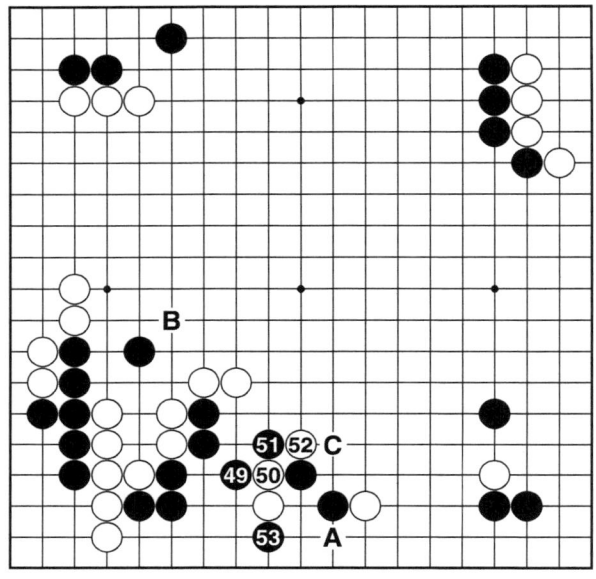

(49 – 53)

49 Black cannot extend to A as White would take the vital point at 49. Common sense requires Black to reinforce his group. However, AI recommends playing at B to focus more on the center than hanging to the stones at the bottom.

52 The cut is a consistent continuation of the invasion.

53 This attachment is a mistake. Black should simply play 1 and 3 in the variation to get out into the center. White has to defend the cutting point with 4 and Black moves out at 5. White 6 secures one group and Black 7 takes the base of the other. This fight is not bad for White, however, Black is slightly behind and must not back down with a move like 53 in the actual game.

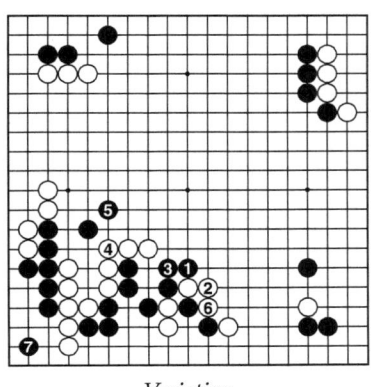

Variation

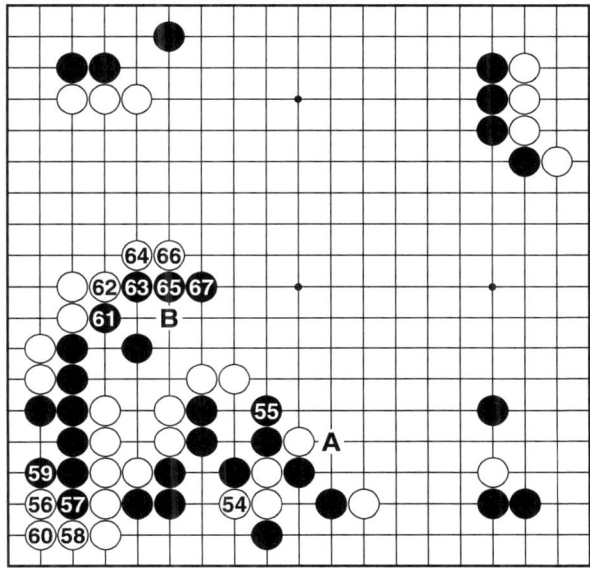

(54 – 67)

54 Both players place too low a value on the center. The recommended play by AI is the atari at 55 and then 56 in the corner. Then, when Black starts running, White can extend at A.

60 At this point White is ahead by about two points.

61 Black should run with the kosumi at B.

62 This is not the best move. If White plays the keima at 64 and Black attaches at 63, White would not play 62 but extend to 66.

67 Black cannot allow White to hane at this point.

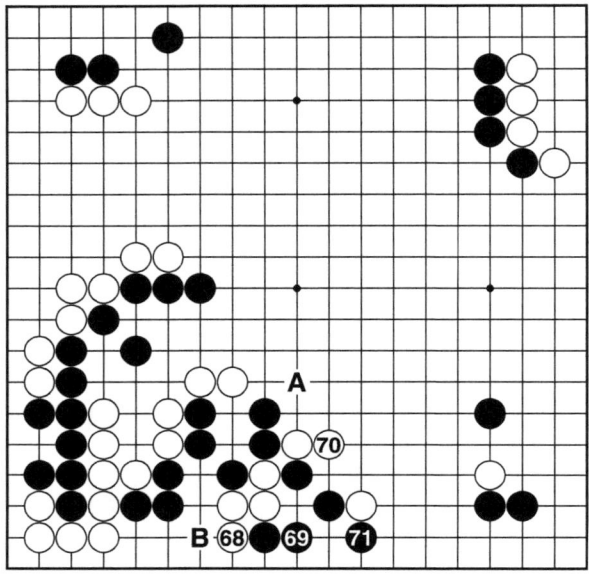

(68 – 71)

68 The fighting shifts back to the lower side of the board. The situation is difficult here with many variations possible. This move is important if you want to keep the threat of A alive, which would seal Black in.

69 This is the wrong direction. Better for Black to take a stone on the outside as shown in variation 1.

71 A big mistake. Black should play B. White can live at the bottom, as in variation 2, while Black gains strength on the outside. Hence, it's better for White to sacrifice the four stones. The move in the game is a loss, giving White a lead of more than ten points.

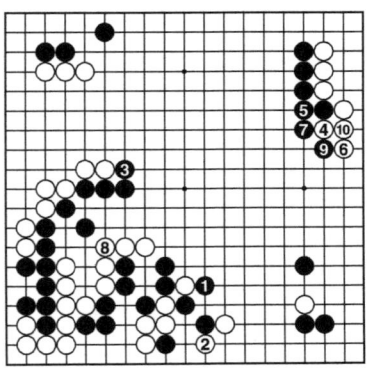

Variation 1

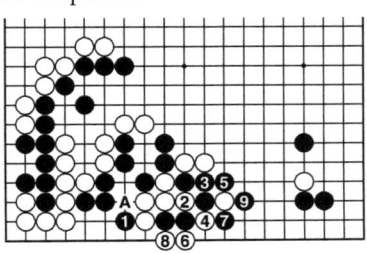

Variation 2

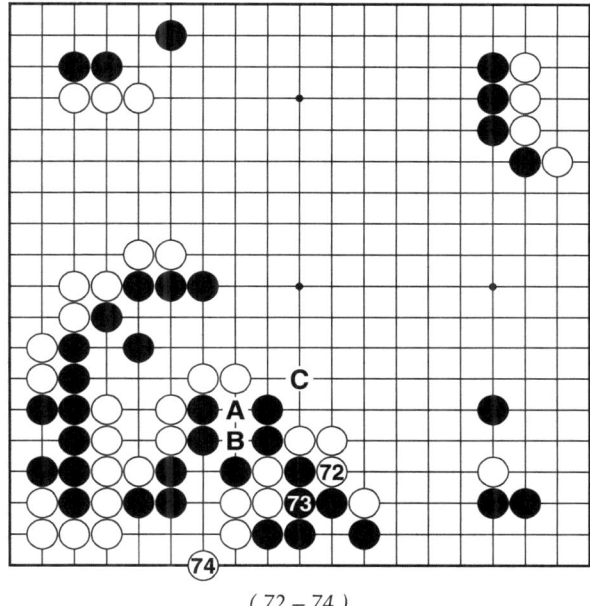

(72 – 74)

72 Another big mistake! The loss here is estimated at about eleven points. White should exchange A for B and then close Black in with C. Black is forced to capture the four white stones as shown in the variation. He cannot allow his stones to be captured. White builds a strong wall on the outside.

74 White connects his four stones to the group in the lower left corner. At this point the game is about even again.

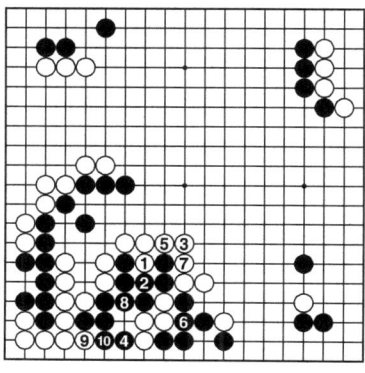

Variation

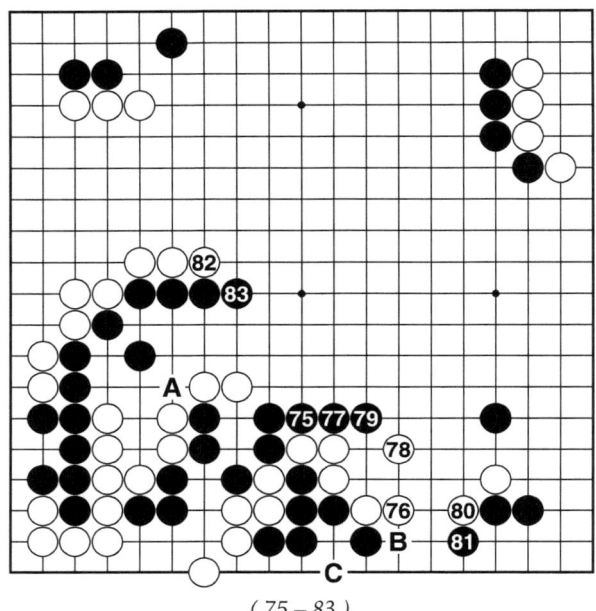

(75 – 83)

75 This move may appear a bit awkward but it is the AI move. It puts pressure against the four white stones at the bottom and at the same time it aims at the cut at A.

78 White must make shape to defend. Attacking at B or C does not work, as Black will play 78 and capture White's group.

79 It's common sense to not allow the opponent a tiger mouth. But in this situation the proper choice is connecting, as shown in the variation. Black is strong and doesn't need to worry. Black 79 is a mistake, giving White an advantage of about two and half points in the game.

82 AI prefers to block at B now, as Black is forced to live at the bottom.

83 Black must extend, as a white hane here would be very painful for him. Even if Black cuts at A, the life of the group is at risk.

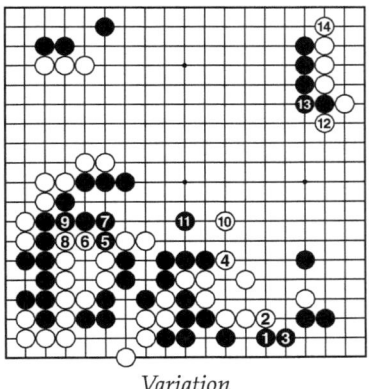

Variation

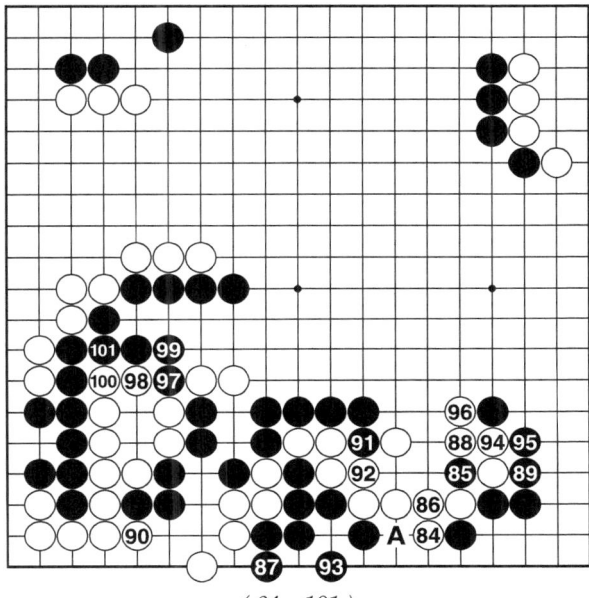

(84 – 101)

84 White blocks to cut off the bottom black group, which is now forced to seek life. White could consider capturing the group at A, but Black would play at 86 and gain compensation on the outside.

87 Instead of making life, Black may consider a trade here in order to sacrifice the stone for outside thickness. The variation shows how Black can seal White in. The question is whether Black can gain sente to play in the upper right corner and seal White in there as well.

88 White takes a stone and threatens to push at 89.

90 White comes back to connect his stones.

93 Black has to make two eyes.

98 These sente moves secure life for White's group.

101 The battle at the lower side is now finished. At this point White is ahead by about five points. Park has to do something to catch up again.

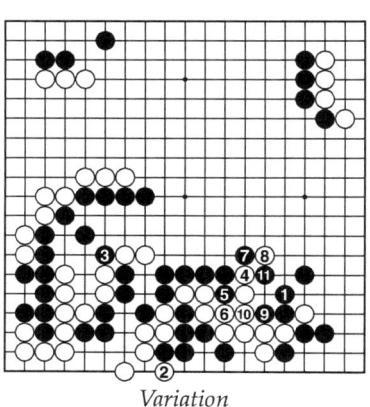

Variation

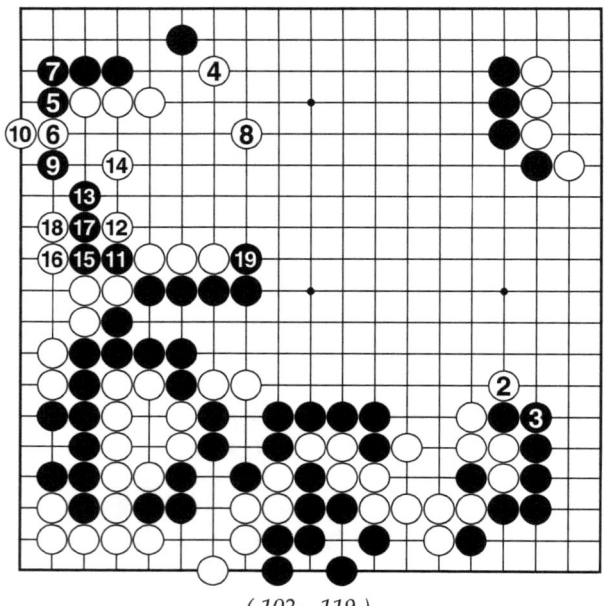

(102 – 119)

102 White has sente, so he plays the big atari 102.

104 This is a point Black would like to take himself in order to enlarge the upper side.

108 After Black 107 there is aji of Black clamping with 109 and breaking into White's territory. The diagram shows only one variation to consider. White 108 allows to extend, after the clamp, to the edge.

109 Park has to do something. The clamp aims at a local fight to exploit a potential weakness.

110 White can extend to the edge due to the defensive move at 108.

111 Black cuts here and White is forced to defend within his own territory.

119 Black gains the bend at the outside, where White has to answer. The downside is the loss of the endgame at 110.

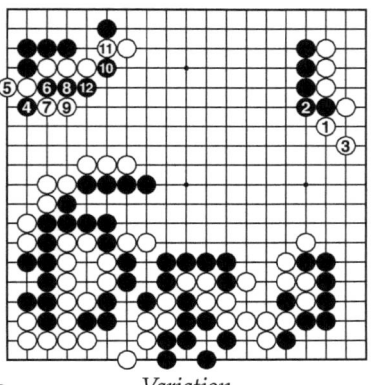

Variation

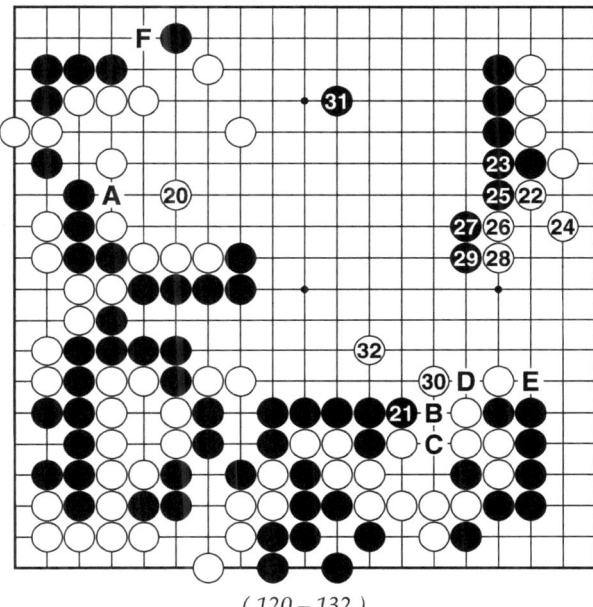

(120 – 132)

120 If White omits the defense, Black can push at A and start a ko.

121 This is the wrong direction. Black should now play the follow-up of the regular joseki in the upper left corner. In the variation, White prevents a black extension with 10 but Black counters with 11 to 15, giving him power to the center.

124 After the tiger mouth in the upper right corner White has a substantial lead of about seven points. Park is again in a situation where he has to create an opportunity.

129 Here Black may consider making use of 121 and play B, White C, and the cut at D.

132 This move attacks Black's group, threatening to rescue the two of White's stones in the center. Simply blocking the right side at E or blocking the upper edge at F are good enough here.

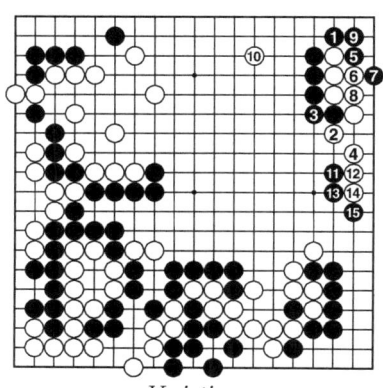

Variation

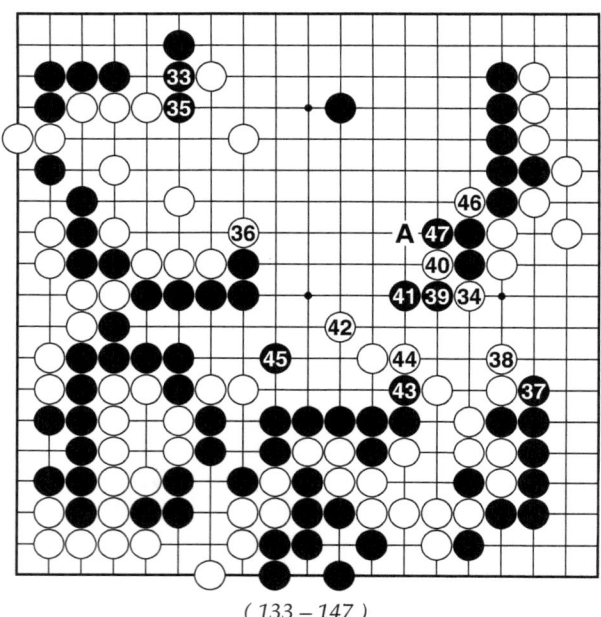

(133 – 147)

133 Black ignores the white keima in the center to push here.

134 Once again we see how the two players refuse to respond to each other's moves. Now it's White ignoring the push at the top.

135 And it is Black again ignoring White in order to push through at the top.

140 A strongcounter attack after the hane, launching the next fight.

142 The kosumi is a double attack against Black's stones below and the two stones at 139 and 141.

143 Black pushes first, in order to create a cutting point before defending at 145.

146 White could choose a simple variation at A, threatening to cut at 146. When Black protects with 2 in the variation, White can take territory in the center, capturing two black stones.

147 Black starts running out.

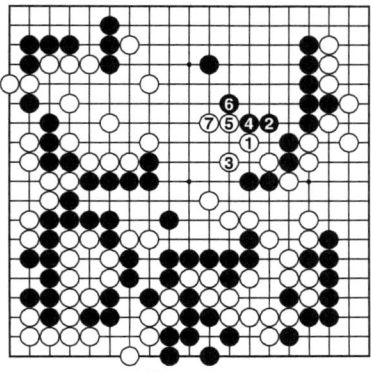

Variation

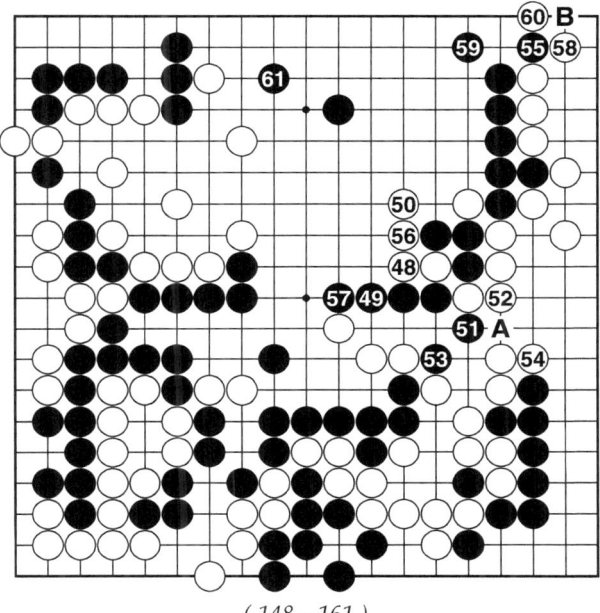

(148 – 161)

150 The net still has a hole, but it's difficult for Black to find a good continuation as two of his groups are in danger. Moving out with 1 in the variation doesn't work.

151 Black exchanges first the atari and cuts in sente.

154 White has to protect here. If he captures at 156, Black can push at A and cause serious damage to White's position.

155 Black cannot start moving out, so he waits for White to decide how to capture the three stones.

156 White captures and is ahead by six points now. It's expected that Shin will bring this lead to a succesful ending.

159 A good technique aiming at a big endgame at B and supporting the upper side.

161 If Black is allowed to cut off the single stone at the top he would gain a great deal of points in this area.

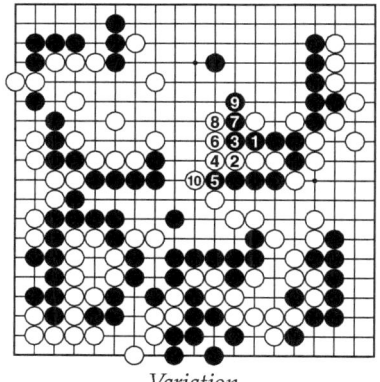

Variation

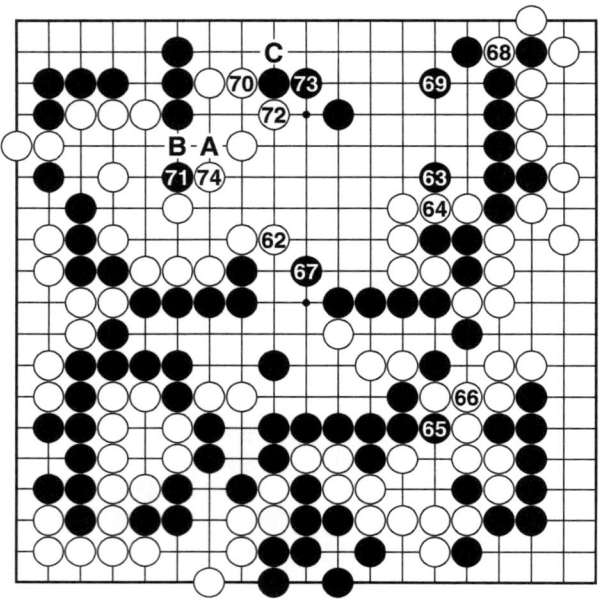

(162 – 174)

162 White doesn't defend immediately at the top, but instead attacks six of Black's stones in the center.

167 Before connecting the stones under attack, Black inserts the atari and the kikashi at 165 and 163. White answers both of them.

168 A big move allowing more follow up moves at the top, which Black must prevent with 169.

170 White finally comes back to defend against cutting off his stone at the top. AI sees White ahead by about five and half points.

171 It was expected that Black would play at 172, White forms a bamboo at A, Black pushes at B, and White finally blocks the area at 171. But Park is in need of an opportunity to do something and sets on a tactic of confusion.

172 Should be better at C and follow the variation.

174 C is still the better choice.

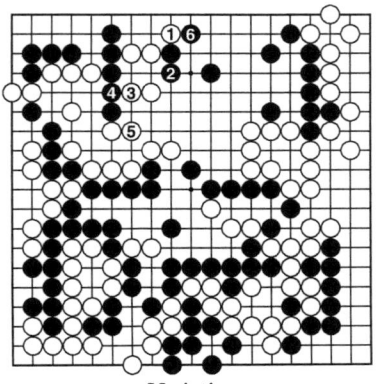

Variation

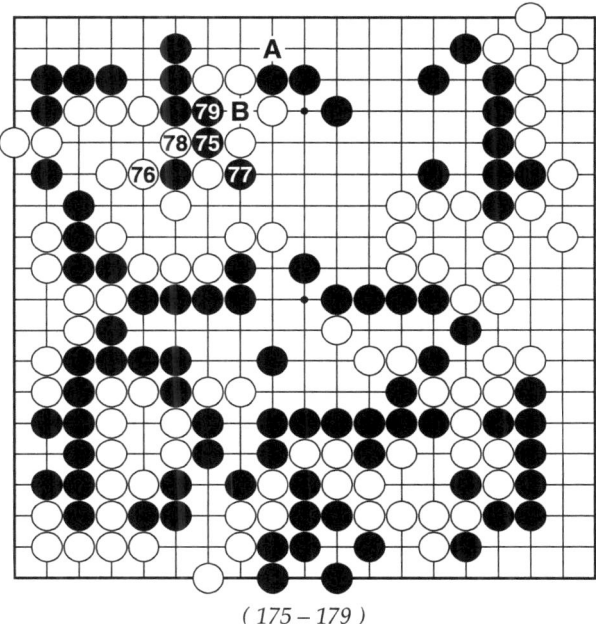

(*175 – 179*)

175 For whatever reason Shin was not aware of what may happen here, if you don't consider your moves carefully.

176 This move is one of the biggest mistakes in the match series. With one move the entire lead has vanished and the game is back to even. Instead of 176, protecting against a cut at 177 would be safe and sufficient for White. The hane at A would be a clever defensive move.

177 Park doesn't need a long time to counter with the atari at 177.

179 This move brings Black into trouble. He cannot simply connect the two stones at B as the variation shows.
Shin now takes a rather long time to think about his next move.

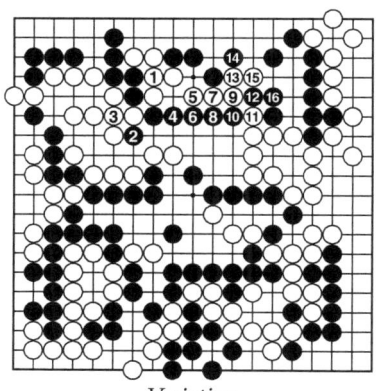

Variation

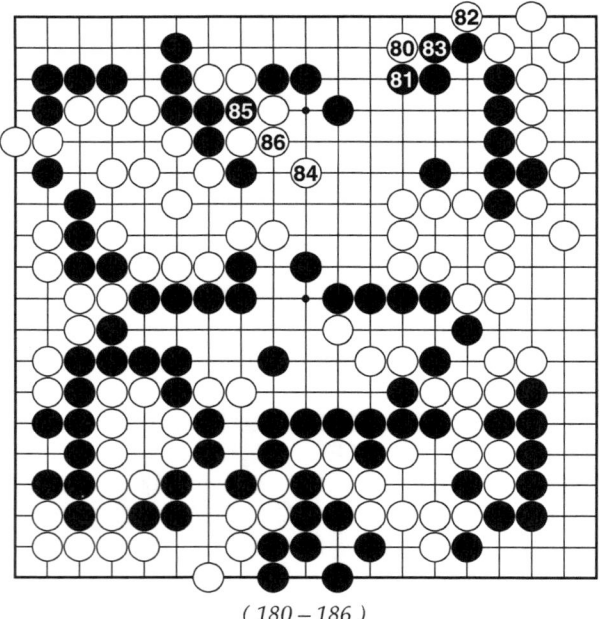

(180 – 186)

180 This invasion sets a trap for Black. If Black answers like in the variation, White is able to connect at 2 and win the capturing race.

181 But Park is aware of the trap and plays a solid answer. At this juncture, Black is leading by about a point and a half.

184 Shin has to limit the damage after his mistake. The game is not over yet.

185 The cut is not only big but also sente for Black. Park has now clearly turned the tables and may look forward to his first win in the Super Match.

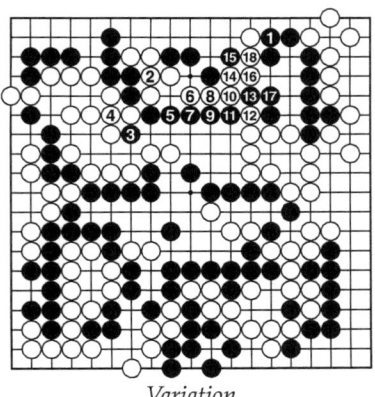

Variation

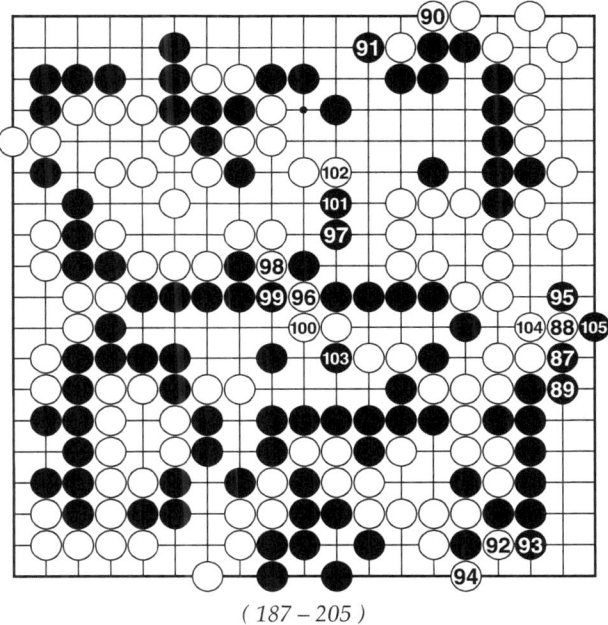

(187 – 205)

187 The game continues with endgame moves.

196 This is a do or die move. Locally it does lose another point. If Black answers correctly he would be ahead by two and a half points.

197 Park is too greedy or simply misjudges the situation. This move is a fatal mistake and should be played at 200. This would be the safe and secure way.

198 Shin cuts through with 198 to 200 instead. Now the eight black stones in the center are cut off and need to take care of their liberties.

203 This move is necessary. White may not be able to capture these stones, but a seki like in the variation would heavily damage Black's center.

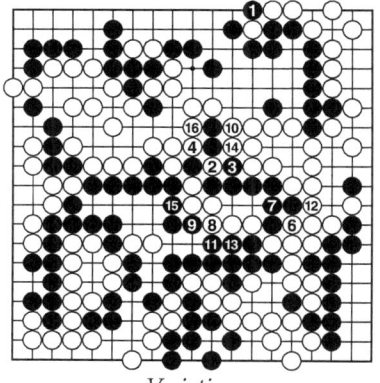

Variation

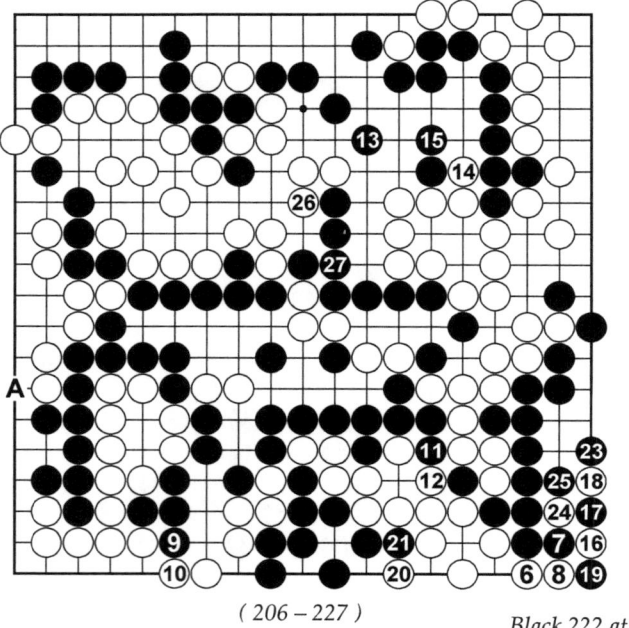

(206 – 227)

Black 222 at 216

206 A big endgame sequence for White. Black cannot block at 208 as a ko fight would be too risky.

212 After this exchange Black must be careful, as White could start a sequence like in the variation. This also shows why 197 was such a big mistake.

227 AI regards a move at A as the biggest endgame for both. For Black it's clearly sente. If White is allowed to play here first, he will save several defensive moves. These will otherwise be necessary due to the presence of the five black stones above.

The next two figures show a close endgame.

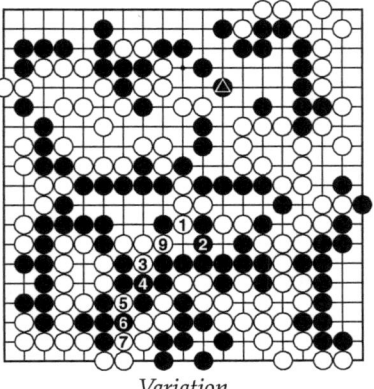

Variation

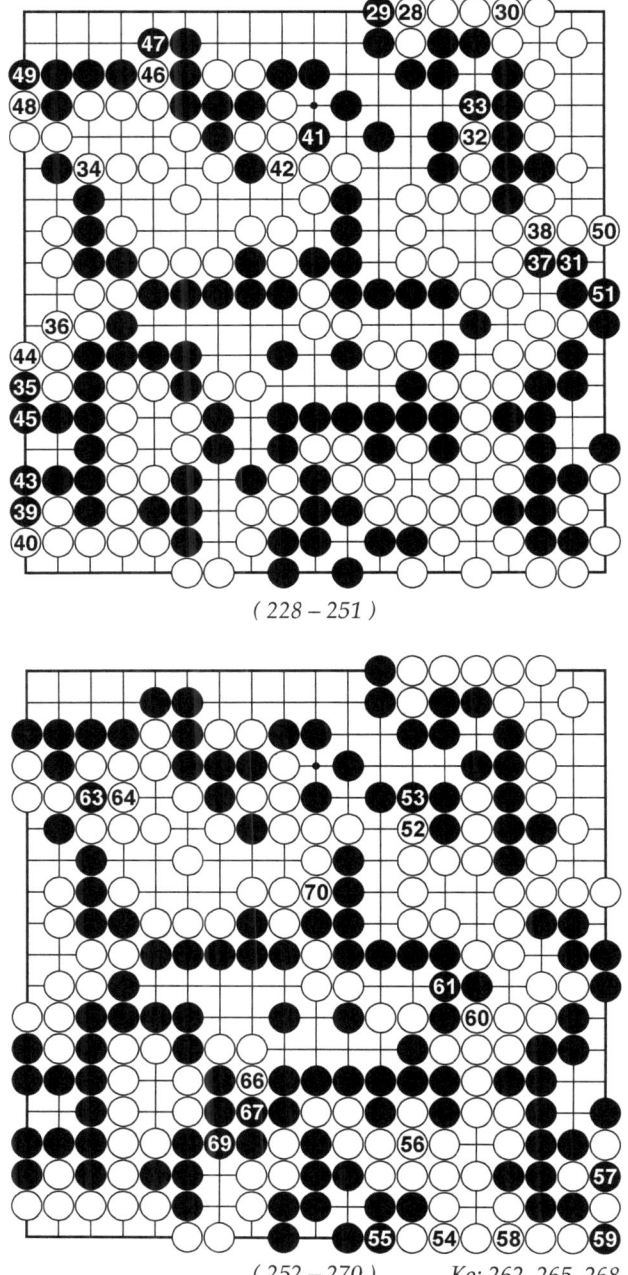

(228 – 251)

(252 – 270)   *Ko: 262, 265, 268*

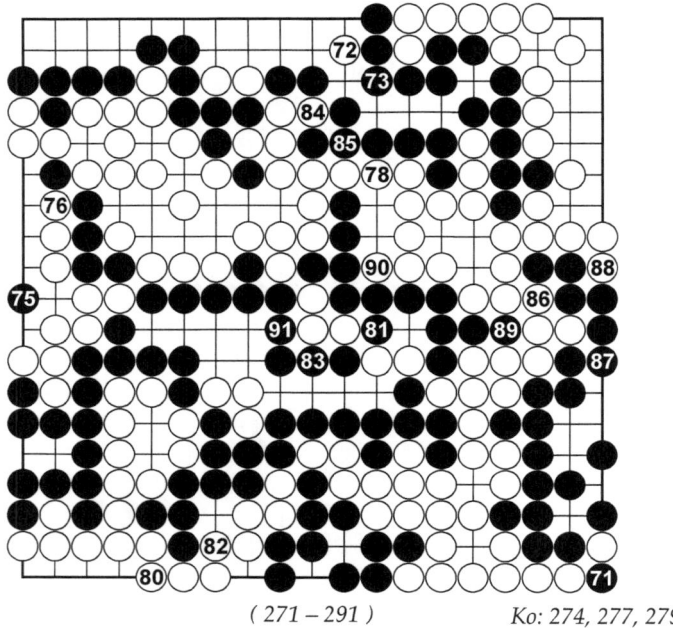

(271 – 291)   *Ko: 274, 277, 279*

291 This is the final move. Thereafter both players occupy neutral
points before counting.

Shin wins this game with 0.5 points and thus the fourth game in the
Super Match series.

Maybe the 3-0 defeat placed some sort of pressure on Park Junghwan? Now Park is in the situation where he is irretrievably behind.
Still, it's a match that requires him to continue until all seven games
are played. Such cruelty hadn't been foreseeable.

FIVE

● **Shin Jinseo**   ○ **Park Junghwan**

Date: 2020/11/16
Venue: Nodo Island of Literature
Time: 90 min plus 5 × 1 min, Komi: 6.5

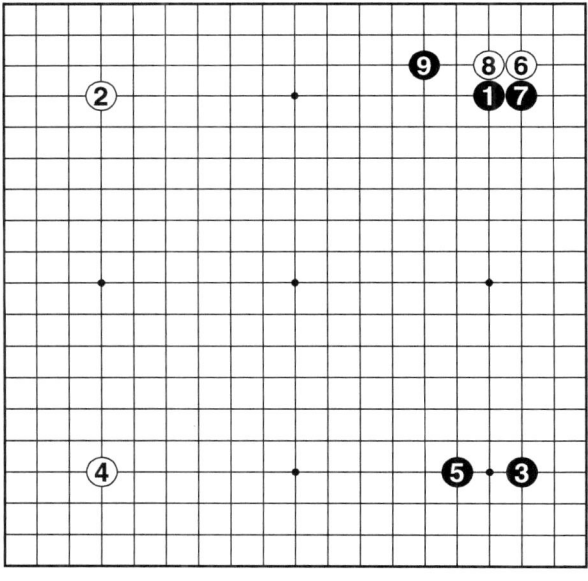

(1 – 9)

Nodo Island, the entrance of Aenggang Bay, is known as a popular fishing spot with an excellent view of the coast. It's the island where the 17th century Korean novel set in Tang Dynasty China was written by Gim Man-jung (pen name Seopo) during his second time in exile on Nodo. The novel has been called one of the most beloved masterpieces in Korean literature.

9   This time, it's Shin who is inviting the Flying Dagger Joseki. Among the modern AI joseki, this is the one with the most numerous and complex variations possible (see annex on page 135).

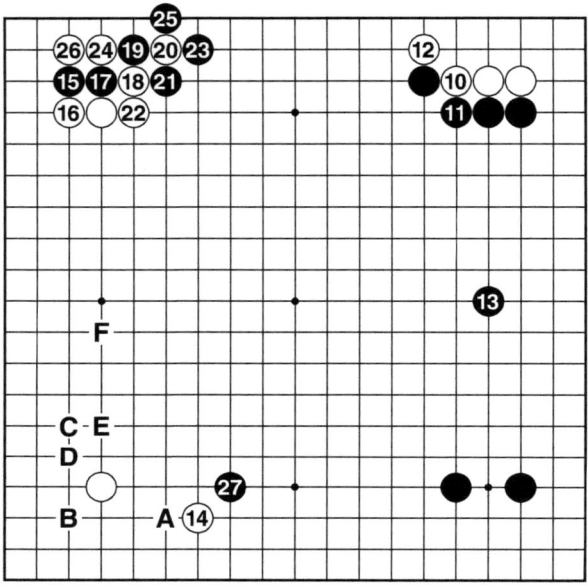

(10 – 27)

10 Park refuses the invitation and opts for a simple way to play.

13 Approaching the corner in the lower left at A and invading at B are both valid options here, too.

18 White opts for a joseki which takes the corner and emphasizes the left side of the board.

27 This move is in line with the AI way to continue. A kakari at 1 as in the variation would be a bad choice. White could first kick at 2. After Black extends with 3, White's pincer at 4 works well with the wall in the upper left corner.

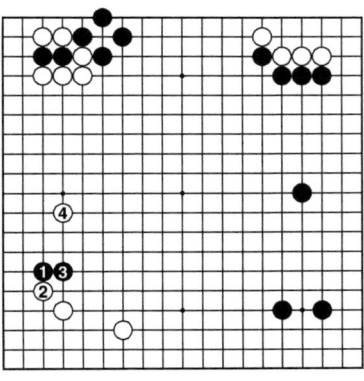

Variation

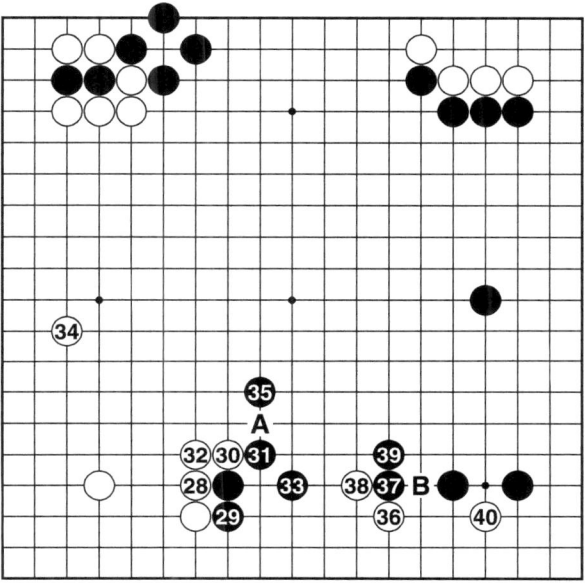

(28 – 40)

29 A one space jump into the center would be worth considering here as well.

32 This is a pretty solid move. It was expected that White would play the double hane at A to gain more influence in the center. The AI is recommending to attach the shimari at B in order to start fighting immediately. This seems not to favour Park's strategy.

34 Again a peaceful move to build a position before entering the opponent's sphere.

35 Black's area on the right side looks very impressive, but in fact AI considers the result to be even.

36 White finally enters Black's area. After the attachement of Black 37, Park took a long time to think of his next move. All of the moves which followed were played rather slowly, as many variations had to be considered during this fight.

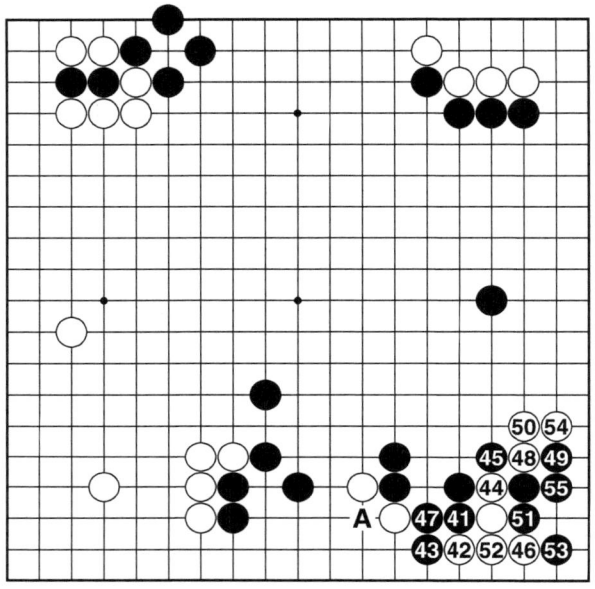

(41 – 55)

41 Black has various options to answer the peep at 40. A simple way could be Black 1 in the variation. Maybe Black did not like White playing 3 instead of 2, with White taking the corner while Black captures two stones and gets a bit overconcentrated. In the game Black therefore blocks at 41.

43 After White's hane Black should connect at 44. White builds a base with 46, the atari at 51 is sente, and Black could cut at A. This way White would not only be sealed in, but also live very small.

46 The sequence from White 46 up to Black 55 follows the AI recommendation.

55 AI sees White ahead by about two points.

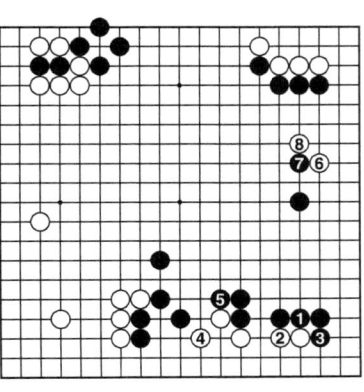

Variation

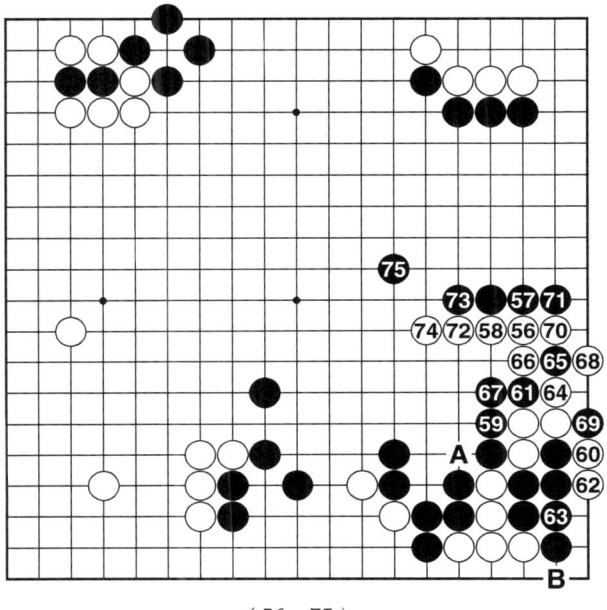

(56 – 75)

56   White has to build a base here. He could attach at 57 or play the
       sente move at 60 and then jump to 71. In the game Park opts for
       the plain jump to 56.

59   This move is neccessary to defend against a White cut at A.

60   This move is not good timing. White should hane first
       at 67 to build a better shape. Black 61 punishes this mistake
       immediately.

62   Another badly timed
       move. White should first
       play at 64 and wait for
       Black's response. If Black
       connects at 67, White can
       atari at 62 without losing
       the two stones on the first
       line. In case Black counters
       with double hane, like in
       the game, the variation
       shows why Black cannot
       easily block at 10.

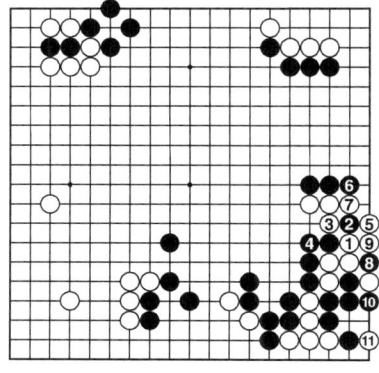

Variation

71   Black now is ahead by
       about a point and half.

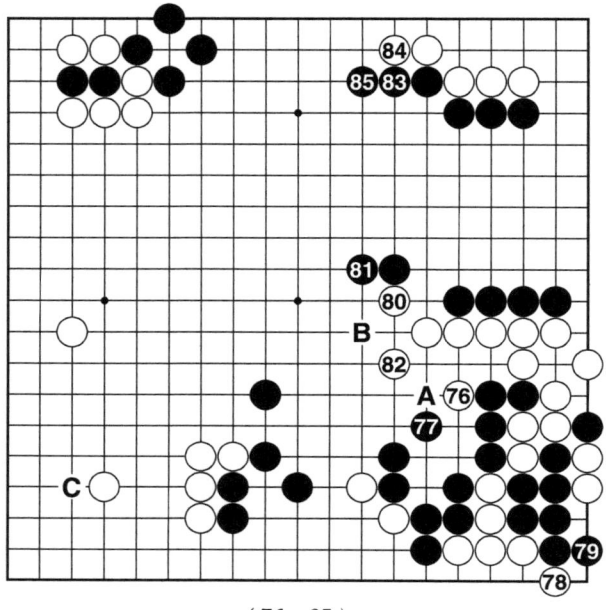

(76 – 85)

76 White eagerly seeks a second eye. However, the better move here is attacking at 77. Black cannot counter at A, as the squeeze at 76 would be severe.

80 White needs to defend his group, but whatever he does Black will take sente. If White plays the bamboo at A, AI would see Black shifting right away to the upper right hand corner. If White jumps at B, Black would attack at C. No player would want to be give away sente without reason.

81 Black's response is calm.

82 This move secures eye shape, but it's quite timid. The AI valuation drops by another two points in favor of Black. He has accumulated a five point lead already.

83 Black seems to have not liked the AI variation shown here so much. He doesn't want to trade.

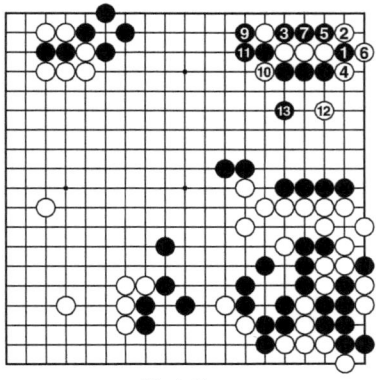

Variation

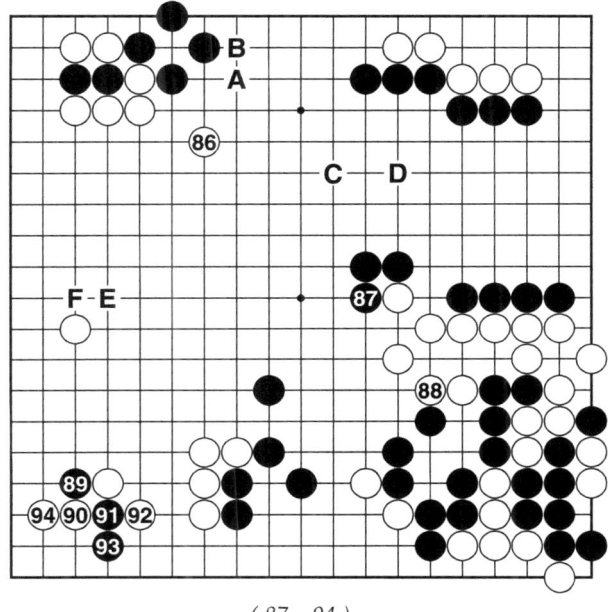

(87 – 94)

87 A thick move, but the top area can still be reduced by the sequence White A to D.

89 It's time to shift fighting to the left side. It's a difficult choice whether to erase White's framework or to invade. Shin took his time before deciding to attack in the lower left corner at 89. Black aims at a local fight in the corner, allowing him to take sente to erase the upper side later on, either at E or by attaching at F.

91 The cross cut is the natural move.

92 Every go player is familiar with the rule of thumb that after a cross-cut, you should extend. In the actual position, AI is in line with the common sense. White should extend like in the variation and the sequence to 13 looks reasonable. Black could consider connecting at the edge with A to I, too.

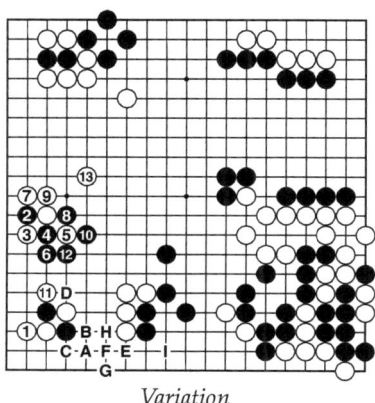

Variation

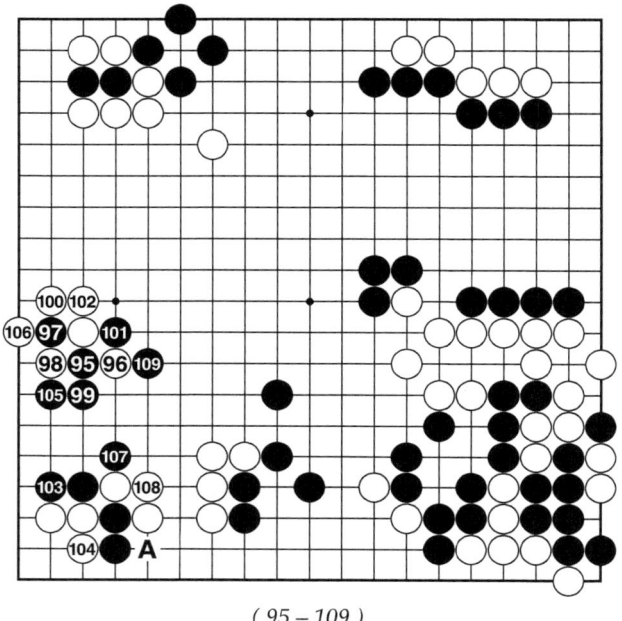

(95 – 109)

97 A cross cut at 101 was expected here. White has to consider his answer carefully in order not to end up with the variation. Black 7 is a famous tesuji attributed to Honinbo Dosaku. However, AI is not afraid of this variation, actually favoring White here.

104 The common answer would be at A. Park decides to block in the corner, providing a slight advantage for the local endgame.

109 At this point Black is ahead by about four and a half points.

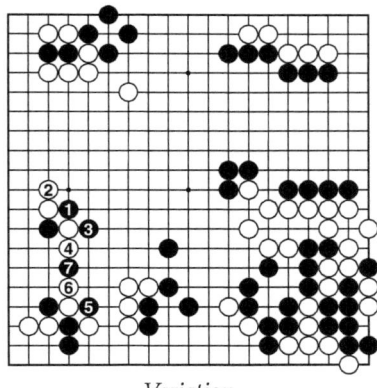

Variation

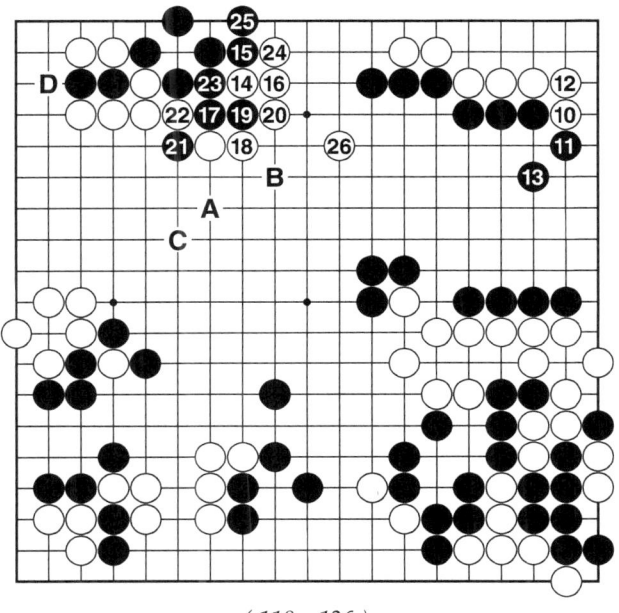

(110 – 126)

113 This move looks natural and solid. However, AI has its own cruel judgement. This move is a mistake, counting for a loss of three points. Black should attach at 118 to help his group at the top.

114 White attacks Black's group to build influence in the center and to reduce Black's area. The sequence up to 125 is almost a one way road.

115 Black could simply live with a move at 123. This would allow him a forcing move around A later on.

126 How to defend the cut? The AI move is B. But the left side is wide and Black can simply start a reduction at C. There is aji at D as well.
The variation shows that White cannot connect his four stones. Hence he must defend the cut in one way or another. Park took twelve minutes before placing 126 on the board.

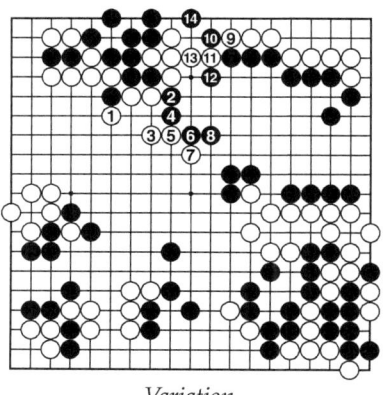

Variation

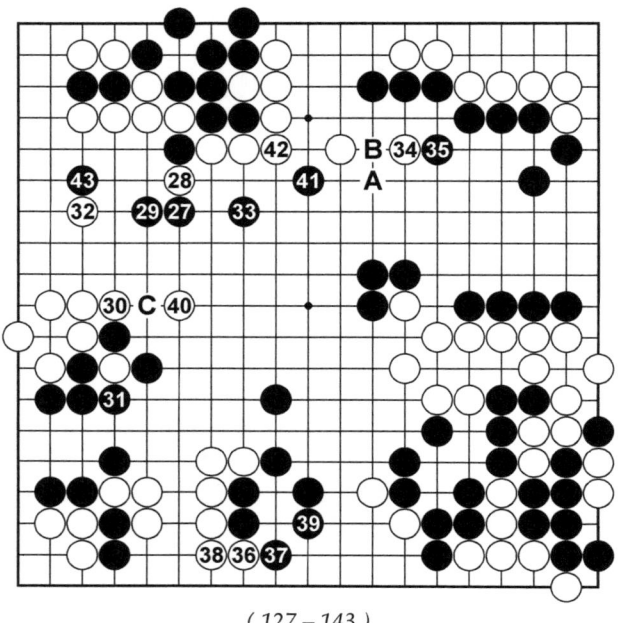

(127 – 143)

127 The fighting is now about the reduction of White's area on the left side.

132 White 128 captured a black stone already, but this move is still necessary to defend against the remaining aji.

135 Black plays a solid defensive move. The AI prefence is injecting the peep at A first, whereafter White has to connect at B.

140 It would be painful for White to allow Black the hane at C enclosing the whole center.

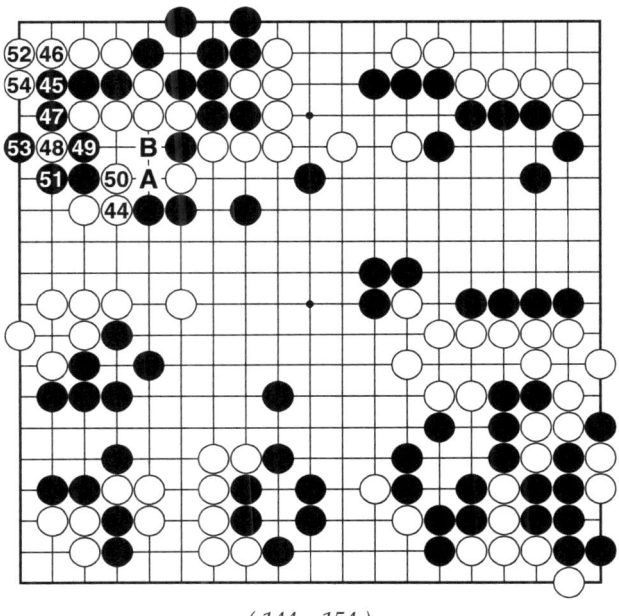

(144 – 154)

144 This move is surprising. Black may simply play the atari at A, threatening to cut off the whole group at the top. When White captures, Black connects at 150 and has managed to dive deeply into White's area.

The better choice for White is shown in the variation, where he keeps all of his stones connected.

145 Black finally draws his two stones out to make use of the aji in the corner.

150 Capturing with 154 does not work, as Black uses the atari at B to connect then at A. So Park goes for a semeai. At this time Park is already in byoyomi.

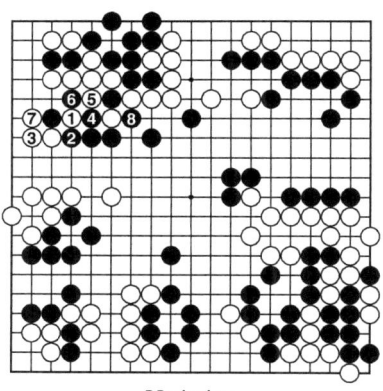

Variation

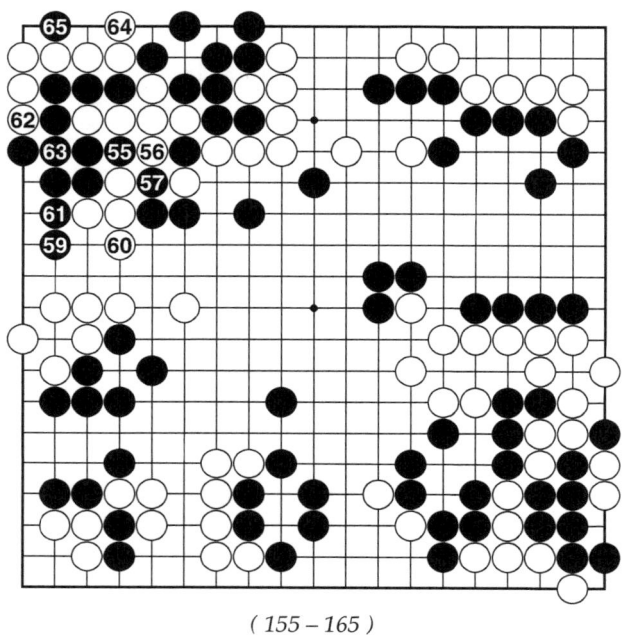

(155 – 165)

155 Moving out at 156 doesn't work for Black. *White 158 connects*
As shown in the variation, White would
win the semeai in the corner and has even time inbetween for
another move in order to connect his other group at the top.
Thus, Shin goes all out by starting a ko.

160 The only way to defend here. If White pushes in at 161, Black
simply captures at 160.

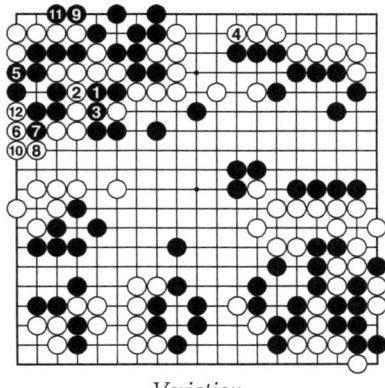

Variation

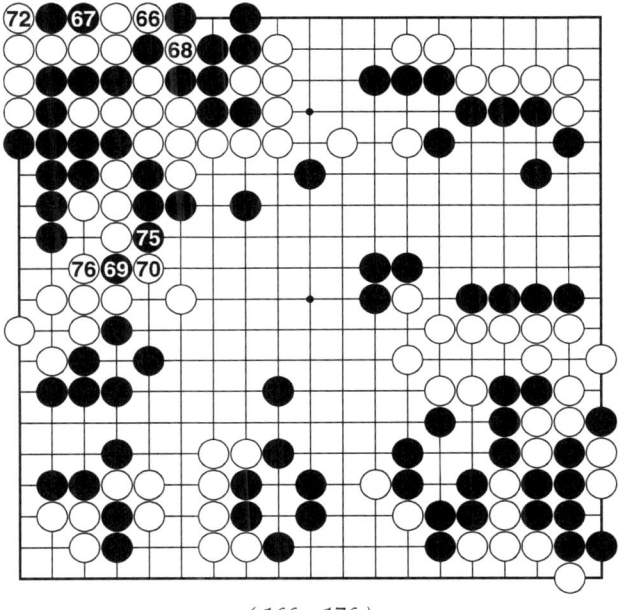

(166 – 176)

166 The ko starts.

169 This ko threat offers a big exchange. Shin must have read that he can capture White's group at the left if White connects the ko.

172 A local ko threat. Black is forced to take a liberty and play 173 inside of White's group.

Black 171 takes ko;
Black 173 at 167;
White 174 takes ko

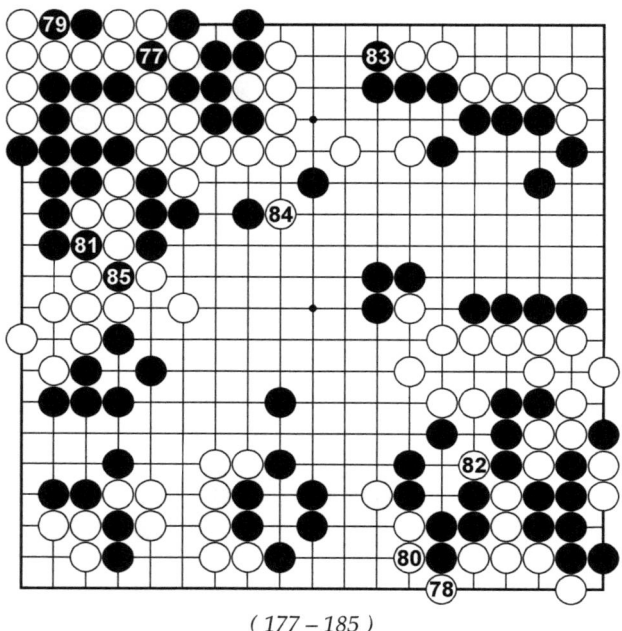

(177 – 185)

178 A ko threat killing the lower right hand corner, if unanswered.

179 Shin doesn't hesitate for long and finishes the ko in the upper left corner.

182 White is in trouble with the two groups on the upper and the left side. This move does not help either of them.

183 Black cuts off White's group at the top.

185 Removing these four stones, Black is strong enough to capture one of the White groups floating within Black's sphere.
At this point, Park resigns.

SIX

● **Park Junghwan** ○ **Shin Jinseo**

Date: 2020/12/01
Venue: Seolri Skywalk, Mijo-myeon
Time: 90 min plus 5 × 1 min, Komi: 6.5

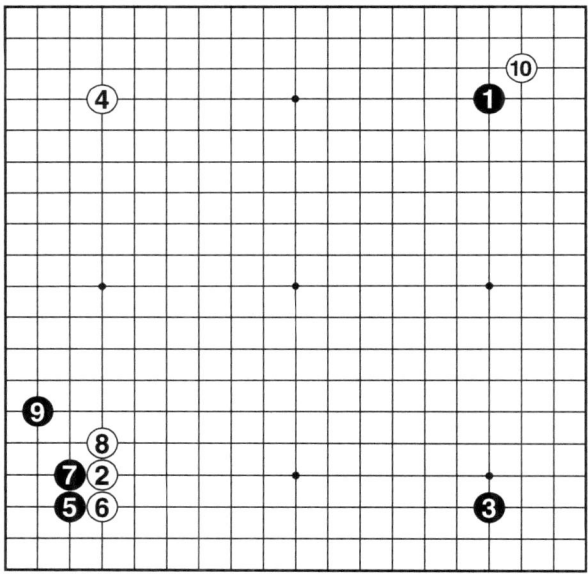

(1 – 10)

The Seolri Skywalk, part of the Treasure Island Coastal View Silk Road project, is the first asymmetric cantilever bridge built in Korea. The opening was held on November 12th with a free trial period ending on 1st December, the very same day Shin and Park played their game here. The swing built at the end of the bridge provides amazing sights over the South Sea and is destined to become another representative tourist destination in Namhae.

9 The opening is reminiscent of the second game, where the same popular joseki was played but in the upper left corner.

10 The moves up to here were played quite quickly.

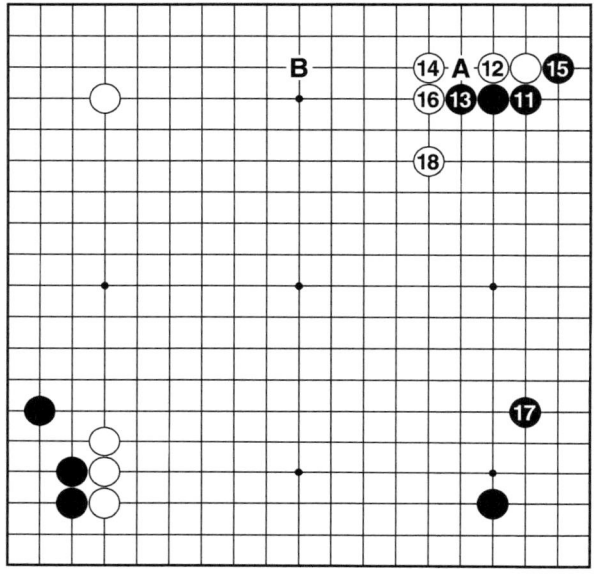

(11 – 18)

14 Another variation of this modern joseki. This pattern is a common modern opening.

15 The usual continuation for Black is a move at 16 or pushing in at A. Tenuki would also be possible, e.g. to form a shimari in the lower right corner. The hane at 15 is, at the time of writing, less common. Its usage was growing in the course of 2020.

16 Following the hane, this is the most frequently seen response. White cannot block in the corner. The variation shows that Black will push and cut. White ends up with two stones captured very early. In addition, the aji of the regular double-hane-joseki has vanished. When this joseki appears at a later stage of a game, White may connect at A.

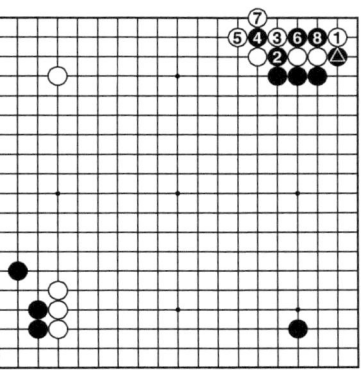

Variation

17 A pincer at B could be considered as well.

18 The natural follow-up.

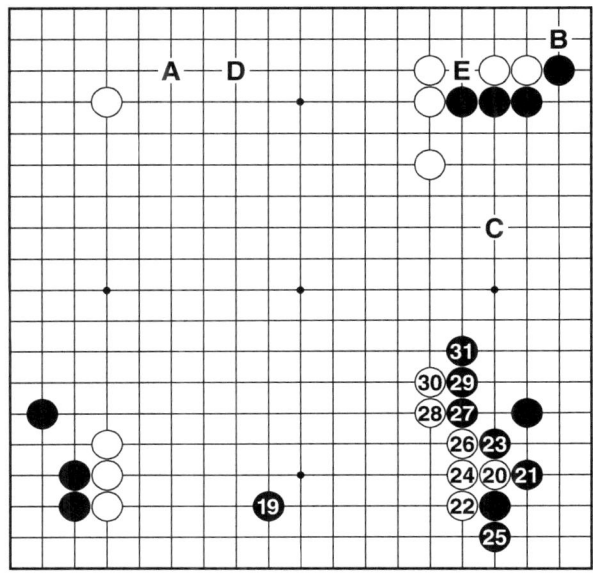

(19 – 31)

19 At this point many options are feasible. In case Black approaches the upper left corner at A, White will exchange B for C and then pincer at D. Black C could also be considered, but Black's corner is not in danger as long as he can push in at E or extend to B for making a base. Hence, it's not urgent to play C. Park may not have liked the 3-3-invasion in the upper left, as this allows White to build two nice walls facing each other on the upper side. Where to play is a matter of taste. Park used up some of his time before coming up with 19 on the lower side.

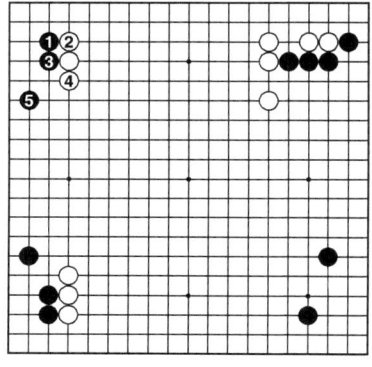

20 Shin attaches at the large shimari. The sequence up to 31 is joseki. White aims at a large scale attack against Black's lonesome stone.

Variation

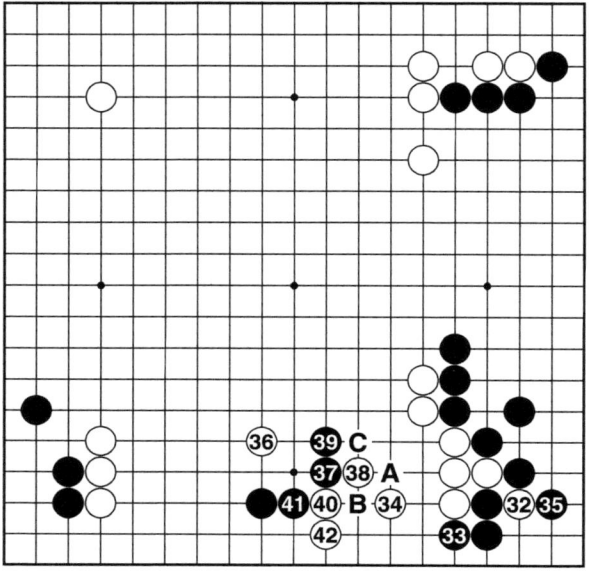

(32 – 42)

32 Shin took five minutes to think about this move. It's good timing. Black has to come back to defend against the aji in the corner.

36 It was expected that White will play the shoulder hit on the hoshi, especially as White has a weakness when Black hits at A. Again, Shin took about five minutes to play the capping move.

37 It took Park only a short time to answer with the keima. He could have attacked more severely at 38, forcing White to defend at A and then extend at B. After a white hane at C, Black could counter with 39. This way he would create a small base within White's sphere.

39 With this move Parks accepts making bad shape. The jump at 1 in the variation would allow him to make better shape.

42 Due to the mistake of 39, AI assigns White a lead of about two points.

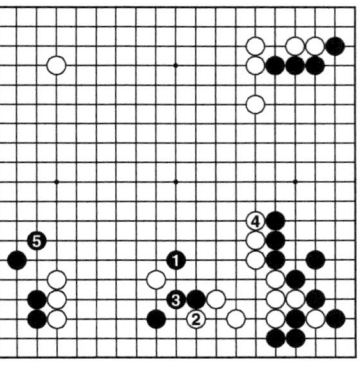

Variation

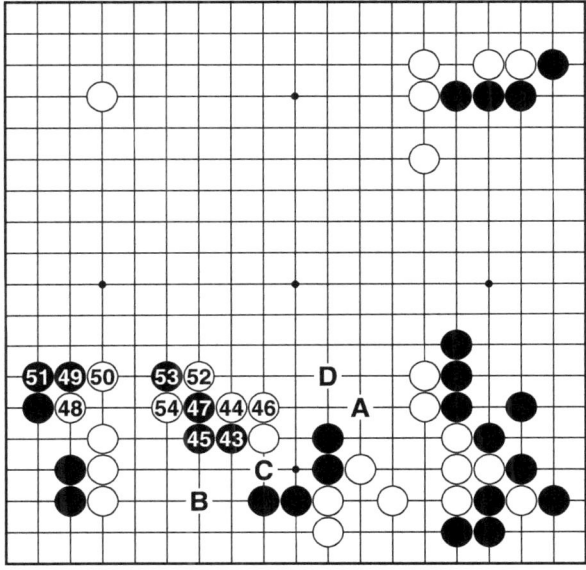

(*43 – 54*)

43 Another doubtful move. AI recommends to move out with A. But it's a difficult choice for White, how to respond.

44 Shin opts for the hane outside, making it hard for Black to get good shape easily.

49 This move strengthens White and weakens Black's stones at the lower edge. Black should simply extend at 51. When White attacks Black's shape, he can sacrifice his own stones on a large scale.

51 At this point White has a lead of about four points already.

52 White should build a base at B. If Black feels forced to answer at C, White can take the good point at D. But 52 and the cut at 54 seem like a slight overplay.

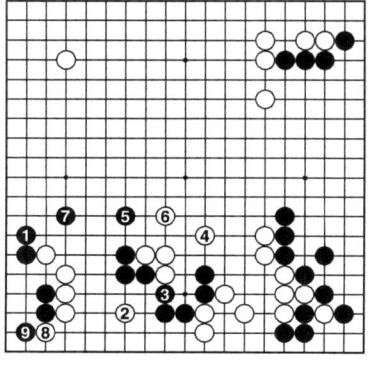

Variation

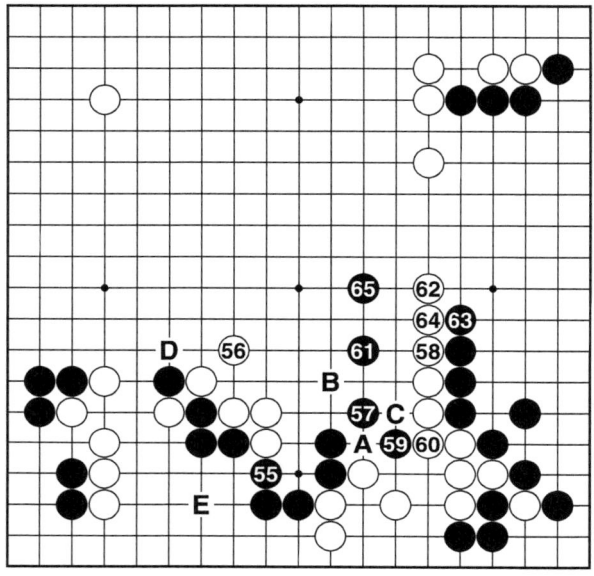

(55 – 65)

55 Fighting has started early this time. Every step now has to be considered carefully, it's easy to fall behind. Black defends the cutting point in bad shape, but AI agrees this to be necessary.

57 Several groups are now on the run.

58 This move might be too timid. White can live with his group as the variation shows. He can even take moves to capture with 3 and reduce Black's area at 7.

60 Another timid move. White could push at A and after Black B cut at C. Shin may have been worried to allow Black to gain sente.

61 Black suddenly has a lead of about three points.

63 Black could keep his lead by extending at D, forcing White to settle his group with a move at E.

65 A mistake. Letting White capture at D is a big loss.

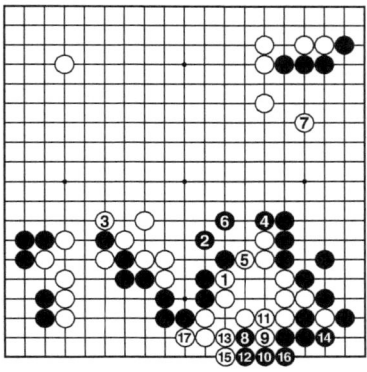

Variation

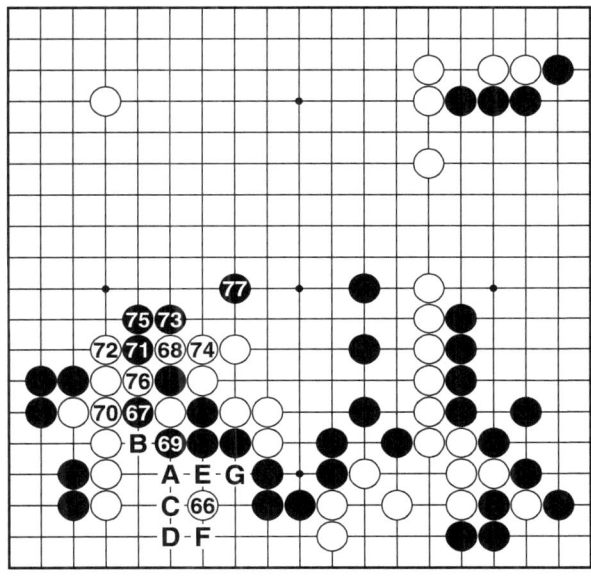

(66 – 77)

66 White should take a stone with 68 to connect two of his groups, but Shin decides to attack Black's shape first at 66.

67 Park, as well, misses the big point. Capturing a single stone is not important now. He should, while attacking White's group to the right, escape into the center as shown in the variation. The game's move is a mistake.

68 White finally bends at 68. However, White could have gained a better shape by extending at 69. After the sequence Black A to E, White could make perfect shape at 68 while Black would need to defend at F. This scenario is preferred by AI, assigning a potential lead of more than five points to White.

70 Cutting at G is not good for White.

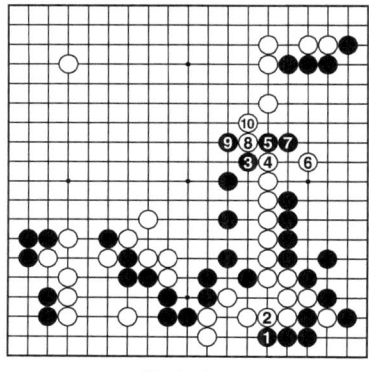

Variation

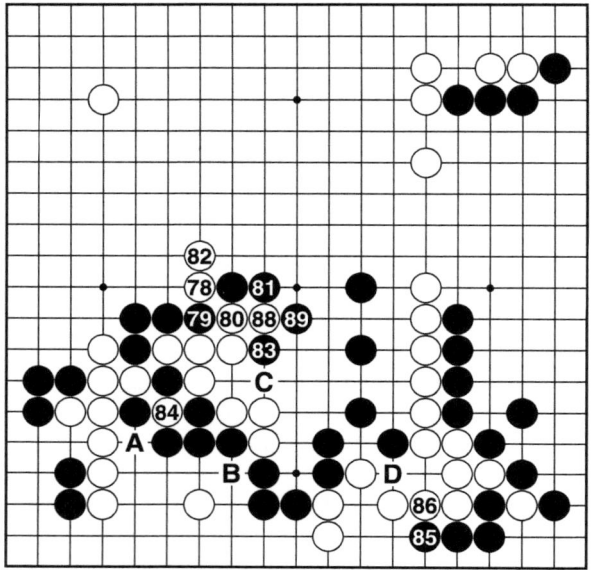

(78 – 90)

Black 87 takes ko;
White 90 takes ko at 84

78   This move at A would safely connect White's groups and
     capture two of Black's stones. Cutting at B doesn't work yet. AI's
     preference is attacking Black's shape at 89.

81   A strong move. Capturing the white stone with 82 would allow
     White an atari at 81.

82   This move shows fighting spirit. However, AI deems this way of
     play unnecessary. It prefers to attack Black.
     The cutting with 78 to 82 is regarded a loss for White. After this
     sequence the resulting position is slightly in Black's favor.

84   The atari at A would be safer and capture two stones. Shin may
     not have liked that Black at 88 would be a sente move, forcing
     him to capture at 84. Black then has another forcing move at C,
     making his group strong in the center.

85   Black should ignore the ko fight but connect at 88 instead. This
     way, White would be forced to finish the ko by connecting. The
     only way Black can win the ko is by capturing the white stones
     in the center. He cannot connect the ko, as White would cut at B.
     Despite the fact that Black cannot win the ko, the exchange of 85
     for 86 was not good for him, as he loses the forcing move at D.

88   White creates cutting points in Black's shape.

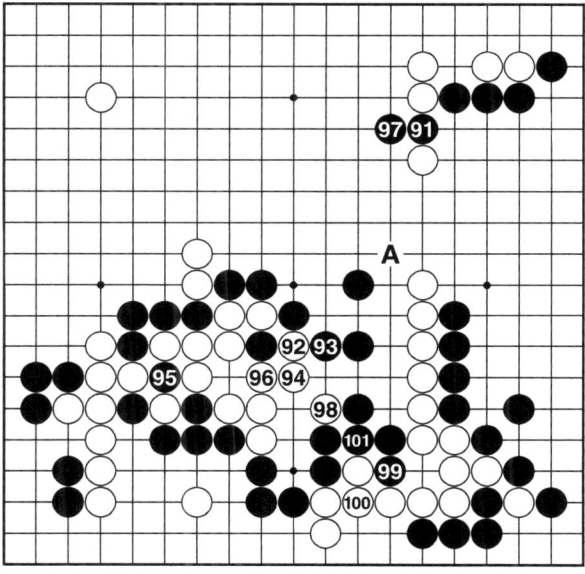

(*91 – 101*)

91 This move looks like a ko threat, but a desperate one. Park seemed very nervous throughout the fighting in this game. Many times he was holding a stone already and bringing it over the point he intends to play, just to stop shortly before actually placing the stone on the board. As he did here for 91 as well. AI recommends a move at A, helping to stabilise Black's group and keep the game close enough for good opportunities later on.

92 Shin doesn't hesitate to ignore 91 and plays 92 immediately. In the following sequence up to 96 he is able to make two eyes and thus be independent of the outcome of the ko.

97 Black has to put hope into his ko threat paying off somehow. He certainly aims at the big White group forming a long chain but having no eyes yet. At this point AI calculates a solid lead of about ten points for White.

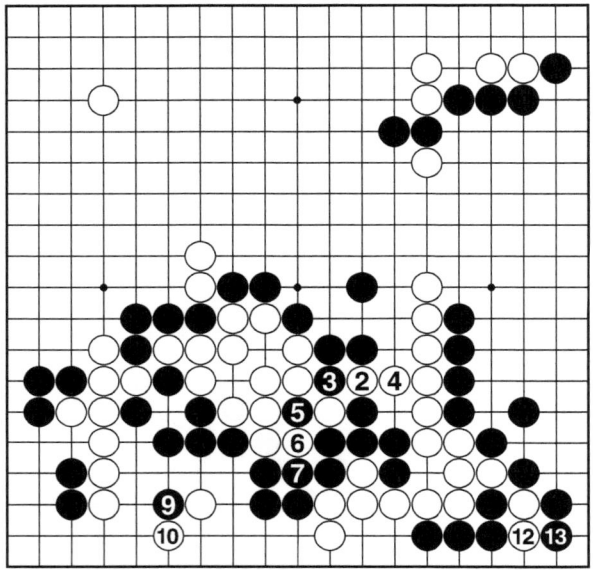

(102 – 113)   *White 108 takes ko;*
Black 111 takes ko

102 Shin is starting the next ko fight. This time it's Black's group
which is at stake.

109 Black has many follow-up moves here to be used as ko threats.

112 A big ko threat for White, allowing him to live if not answered.

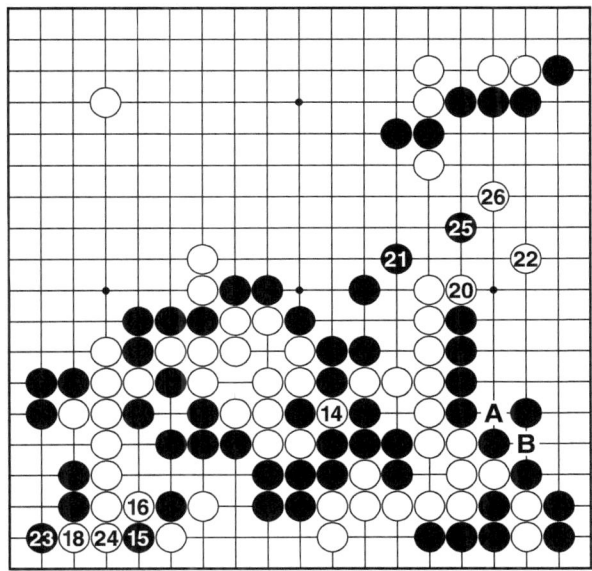

(114 – 126)   *Black 117 takes ko;*
Black 119 connects

117 Black cannot live with his group at the bottom. But every move in the variation can be used as ko threat. If White plays at 3 instead of 2, Black has 2 to force White to connect on the first line with A. Both ways there are some further threats for Black.

118 Big moves threathing to live with the white group are A or B in the figure. The move in the game doesn't gain sufficient compensation for letting Black win the ko. In addition, when Black connects at 114 White's group on the right is under pressure.

119 Black's group is not safe yet, but he can attack White's group and in this way bring his own out of the danger zone.

120 The kosumi at 121 should be played by White first. It's the key point between both groups.

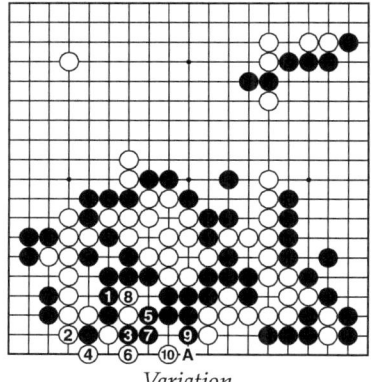

Variation

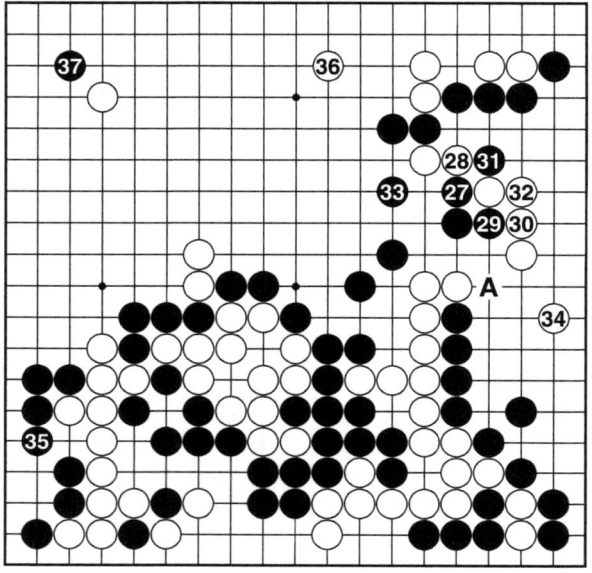

(127 – 137)

128 The fighting here is not easy. White has an eye in gote at the bottom and must now make a second one on the right hand side of the board.

131 Black was expected to cut at 132. Even if being squeezed like in the variation, the result should be playable for Black. The white stones neither have an ideal shape nor position.

133 Black's intention is to help his center group, which is needed to prevent White from using forcing moves against this group to build a moyo at the top.

134 White defends against the cut at A. White is alive.

135 Black takes care of his group in the lower left. A white move at 135 would take over the corner.

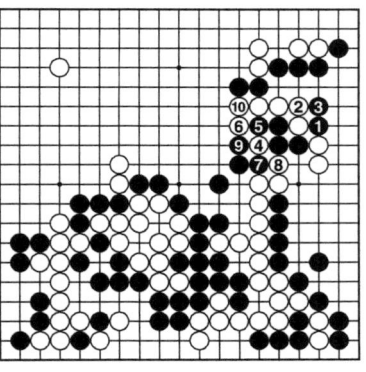

Variation

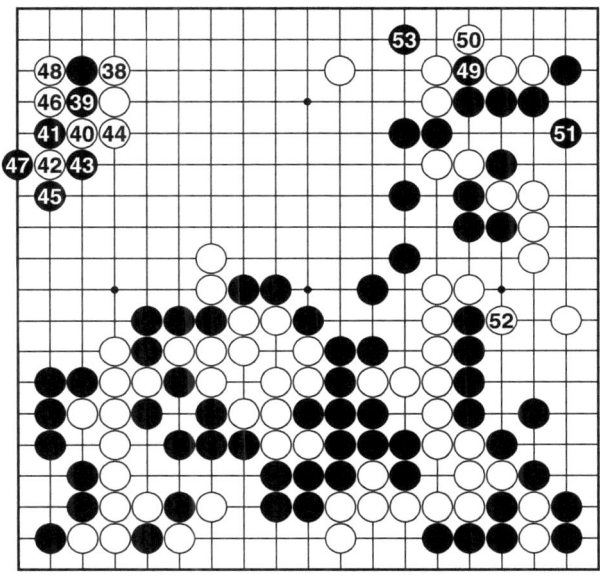

(138 – 153)

138 The joseki after the 3-3-invasion in the upper left corner is played quite quickly.

148 Looking at the overall situation, Black doesn't control a lot of territory and hasn't much chance to gain more, while White's prospects at the upper side look promising. The fight is shifting to the last area where points for territory can be made.
At this stage White has a lead of about seven points.

151 Park spent about eight minutes before adding another defensive move to his group. This may not be necessary, but it's safe.

153 A strong move to invade the upper side. After 1 to 6 in the variation, White must play 7 at 12, allowing Black to hane at 10. White 7 and 9 in the variation end in a disaster.

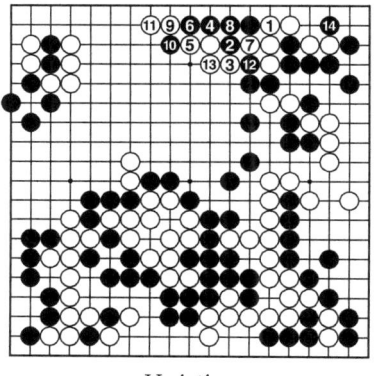

Variation

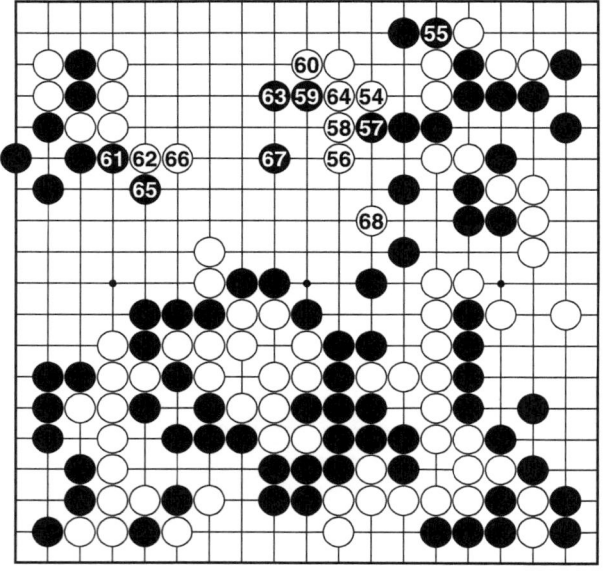

(154 – 168)

154 This move caught observers by surprise. Shin may not have
liked Black to erase the upper side, especially as there is also aji
remaining in the upper left corner. Hence he opts for sacrificing
a big corner in the upper right and go for compensation at the
top.

159 A strong counter attack by Black. The white stones do not have
a base and cannot escape
into the center.

161 At this point the AI sees the
game as balanced.

168 A mistake. But how should
Black punish this move?
The variation is AI's
proposal: Reinforce Black's
position first and then
reduce White's area.

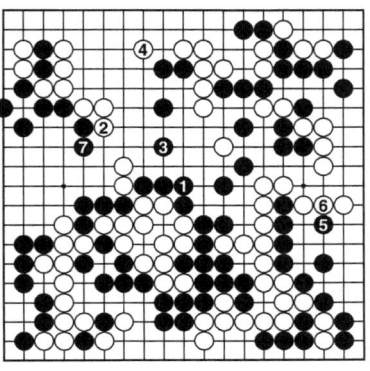

Variation

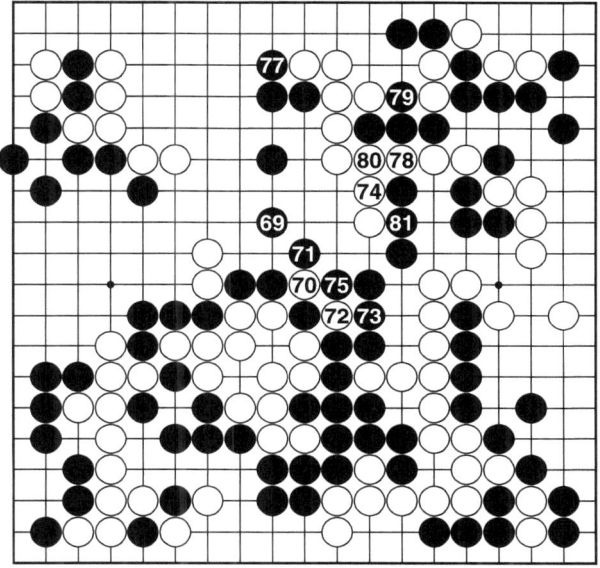

(169 – 181)   *White 176 connects*

169 The game enters a difficult fight. Black has almost separated White's groups and uses the attack to reduce the upper side. But Black has to be careful as his own group is under attack as well.

170 White cuts and aims at splitting the Black group in two.

177 There is the question of whether Black can win the semeai as shown in the variation. Black has more liberties, putting him ahead in the semeai.

178 With each of the following moves placed on the board, the live AI increases the final territory count, starting with a lead of two and a half points for black and building to almost thirteen points after Black 181.

181 It seems Park has found a way to win this game.

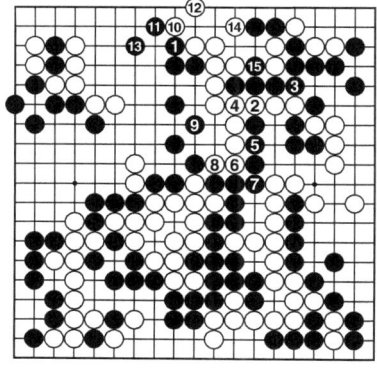

Variation

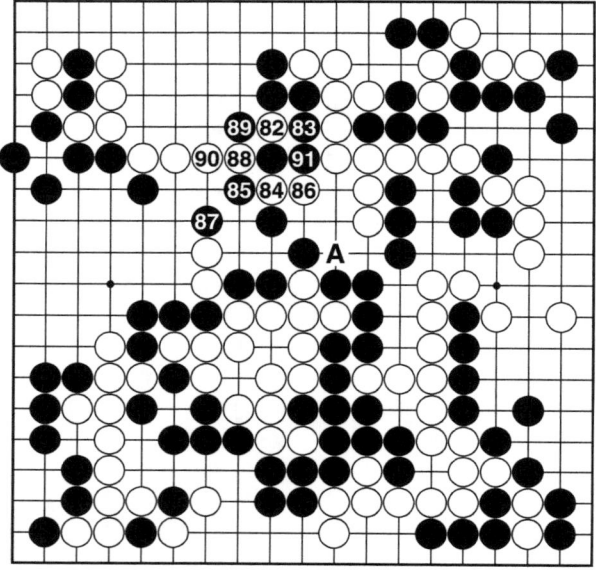

(182 – 192)

182 White starts a counterattack aiming at Black's weaknesses. The
sequence in the variation shows a way to live for White. If Black
plays 13 to prevent a second eye, White can link up at the edge.
However...

187 Black doesn't connect at 5 as in the variation but instead forms a
hanging connection with 187.

188 White cuts on the other
side and the moves up to
191 are forced. Both Black
and White end up with a
group being cut off and
need to win the semeai.
Even more, there is a
cutting point at A.

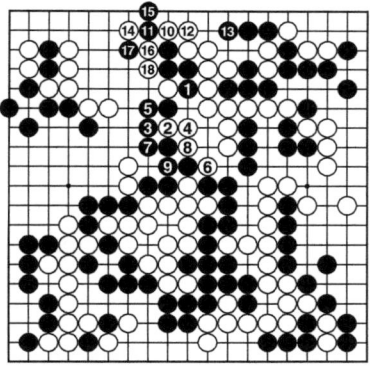

Variation

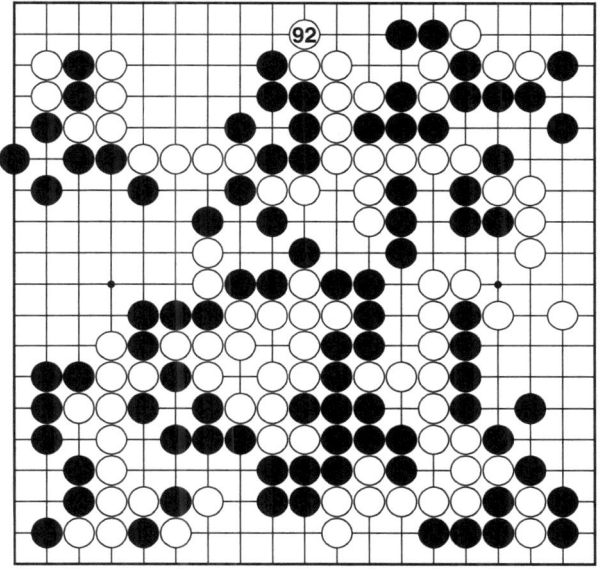

(192)

192 Increasing the number of liberties of White's stones looks
reasonable. At the same time, the move aims at Black's base.
The expected move was White 1 in the variation. The follow-up
shown would be good for White. The tesuji at 7 is especially
noteworthy. In case White plays 7 at 9, Black would counter
with the atari at 7 and then hane at A. White cannot prevent
Black from either making
a second eye or connecting
on the edge.

However, White 1 will
be countered by a black
extension at 4. White is
forced to answer at 2,
preventing Black from
linking up with B. Black
then exchanges C for D
and builds a strong shape
with at 9. Hence, White 1
in the variation doesn't
work.

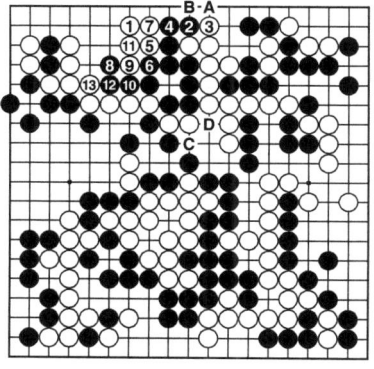

Variation

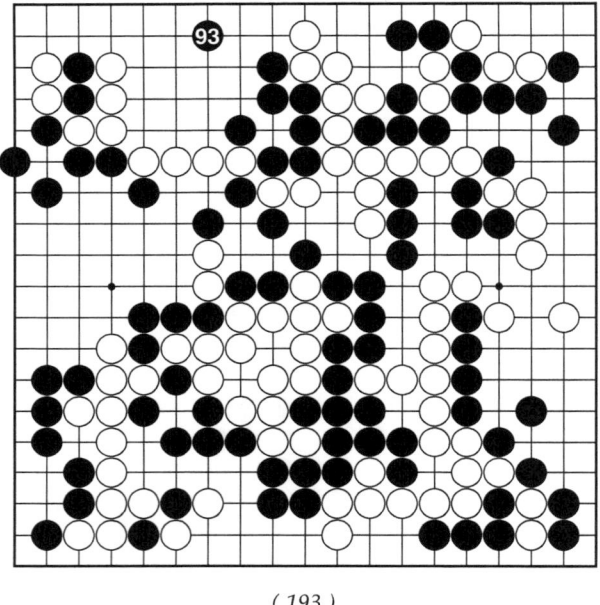

(193)

193 This move is a mistake. Black should have played the atari at 1
in the variation and then followed the sequence up to Black 15.
This way he will win the semeai against White's group and thus
rescue all of his stones.

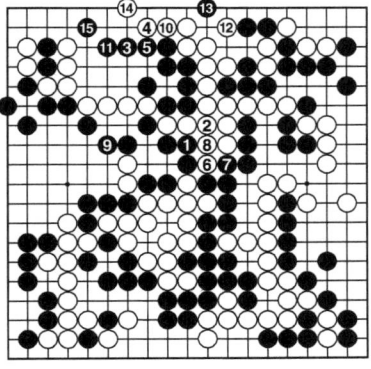

Variation

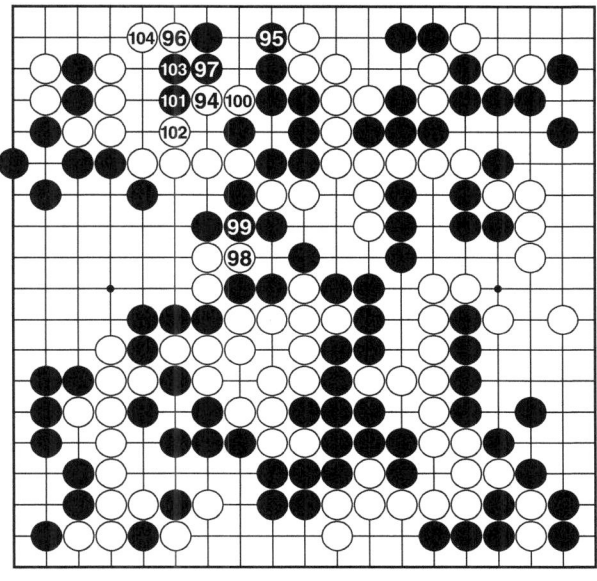

(194 – 204)

194 White misses the chance to punish Black's mistake. White could
win the local semeai with a move at 1 in the variation. Black is
able to rescue his big group by defending at 16. However, it's
up to White now to diminish Black's potential on the left side.
White's lead would be a very small margin of about a point or a
point and a half.

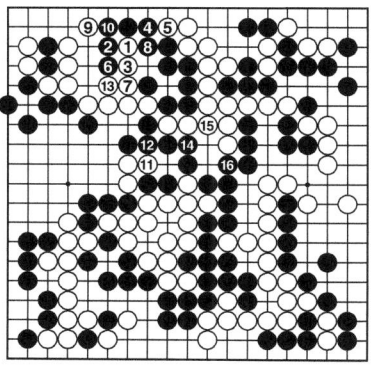

Variation

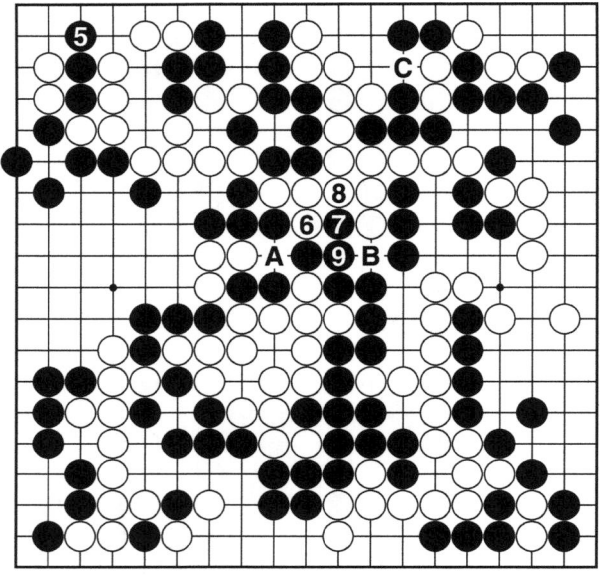

(205 – 209)

205 The last big mistake in the game. Black should have played the atari at 206 first and then followed up with the sequence given in the variation.

209 Playing at A and going for a ko with White at 209, Black 207, White 208, and Black B is not good. White has a big local ko threat at C.

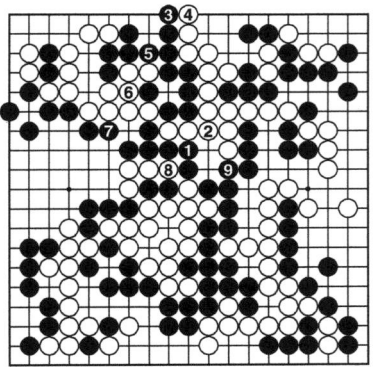

Variation

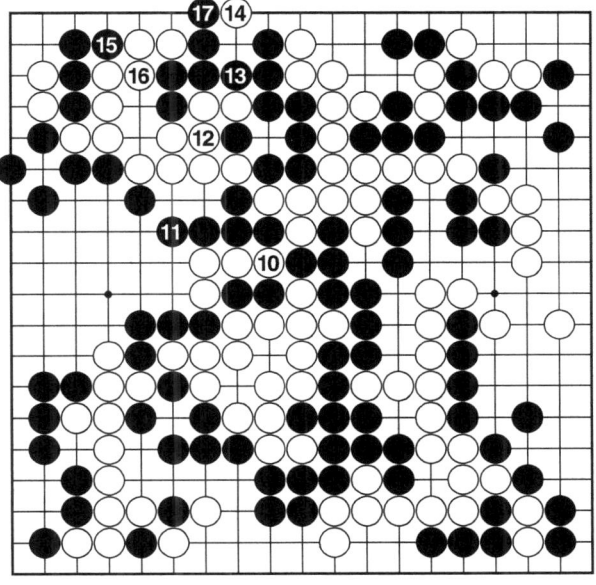

(210 – 217)

210 White cuts off Black's giant dragon. If White survives with his group he will win.

211 Black cannot take a liberty, which would help in the capturing race above, because White can play the atari sequence in the variation. This counter was enabled due to the capture of two of Black's stones in the center. At this point, finally, the live AI at BadukTV again shows a positive score for White.

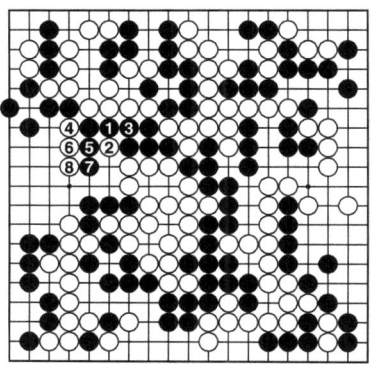

Variation

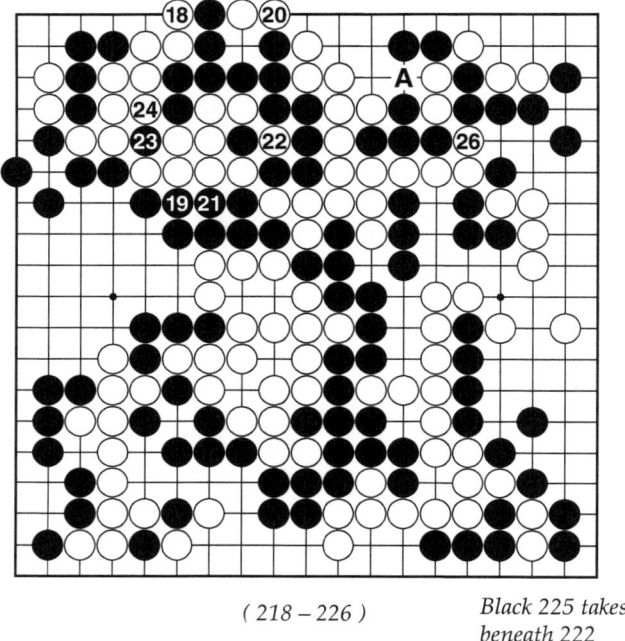

(218 – 226)   *Black 225 takes*
beneath 222

226 Park finally manages to create a ko, but White has the ultimate
ko threat. If Black captures eight stones at 223 and thus kills
another eleven stones in the upper left corner, White takes four
stones at A and kills Black's giant dragon of thirty-three stones.
Here, Park resigns.

SEVEN

● **Park Junghwan** ○ **Shin Jinseo**

Date: 2020/12/02
Venue: Namhae Exile Literature Hall, Gyeongnam
Time: 90 min plus 5 × 1 min, Komi: 6.5

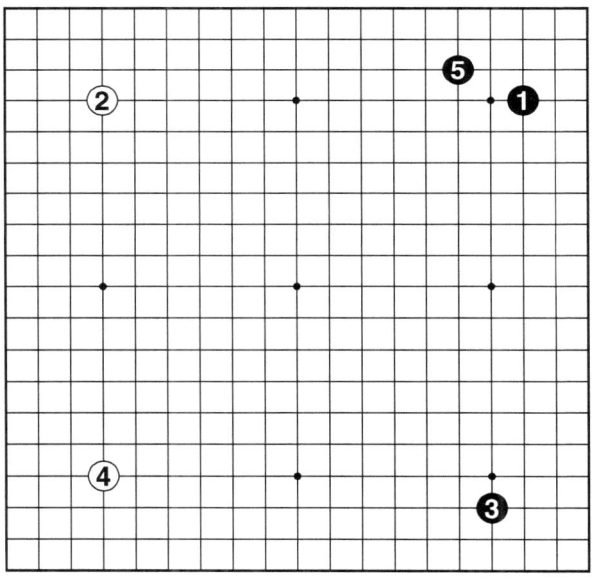

(1 – 5)

The largest of its kind, Namhae Museum of Exile Literatures specializes in literary works of those who lived in exile on Namhae island. Various exhibitions and lectures provide insights into their works.

Here is the venue where the final game of the Super Match series is played. The incredible success of Shin's performance so far may get its crowning glory.

5   For this game, Park chooses a rather traditional opening with two 3-4-points and a regular shimari. Still, this opening is regularly played in top professional games.

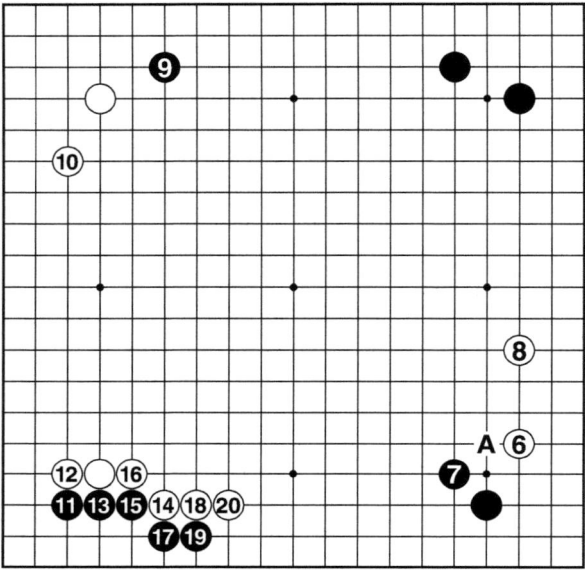

(6 – 20)

6 More common than the low approach is the high kakari at A, followed by the attach-and-extend joseki. Without a doubt the low approach is a regular choice as well.

12 Blocking at 13 would also be possible. After a simple joseki as in the variation, White would be able to play the dual purpose move at 5, extending from the wall and approaching the two black stones in the lower right corner.

14 Once more, the fourth time in this series, the chance to play the Flying Dagger Joseki is given, where difficult variations arise from Black's attachment at 17.

15 And as before, this option is refused to go for a simple variation.

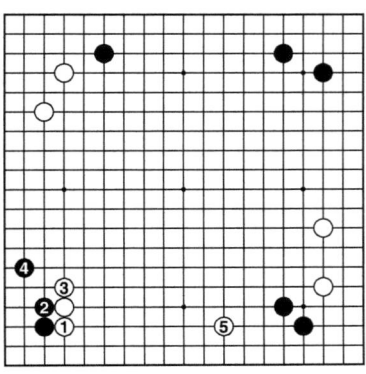

Variation

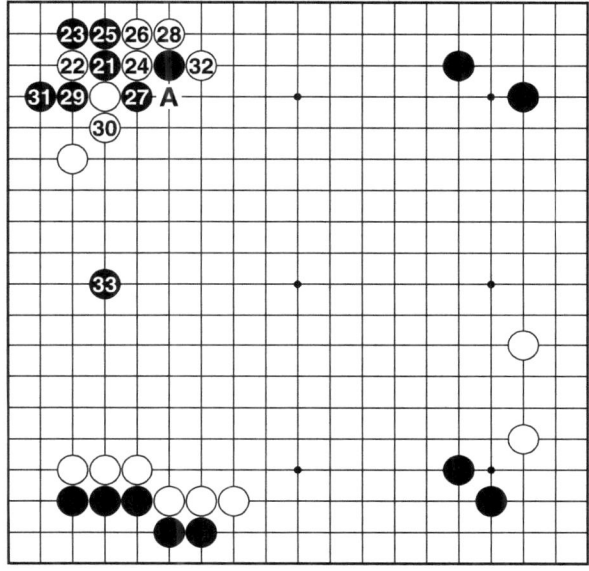

(21 – 33)

21 The attachment is a new AI joseki and has been adopted in regular games. The traditional joseki at 25 would be playable as well.

26 Shin doesn't hesitate to extend at 26. The other main line of the joseki is shown in the variation diagram. After playing 1 and 3, White would like to take the big point on the left side before Black establishes a position there. This, however, allows Black to play the good move at 6, developing the upper side. The joseki played in the game doesn't focus on the left side only.

33 A good move. It would be too early to connect at A, which would allow White additional moves to harrass these two stones.

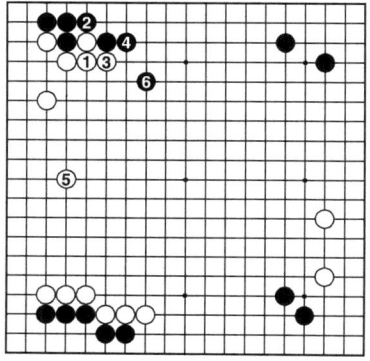

Variation

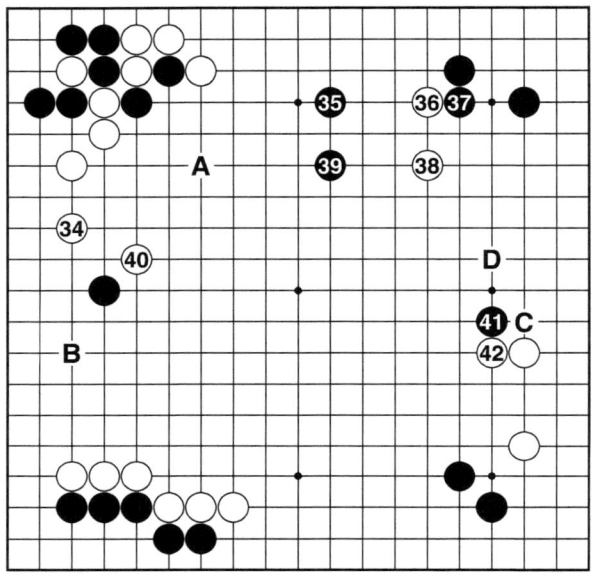

(34 – 42)

34 A move at A was expected to capture the two of Black's stones and settle White's position. It used to be rather common sense to approach the black stone from the lower side at B, as this forms an extension from the lower wall and at the same time denies Black building a base too easily. However, the overall understanding of the game has changed and the small one point jump is appropriate here.

35 A good move. White cannot turn the left side into territory with a single move. Hence Black sets his claims on the upper side.

36 A kikashi to reduce Black's position lightly. An invasion seems not to be a good choice – neither now nor later.

37 A calm response. Black could also attack at 38 instead, starting immediate fighting.

41 Black ignores the attack of White's stones at 40. It seems Park is thinking the stone on the left side can manage and initiates a splitting attack on the right side first.

42 Shin avoids pushing at C and inducing a black move at D. There have not been any bad moves so far, both play rather lightly. Still, AI analysis calculates a lead of about two points for White already.

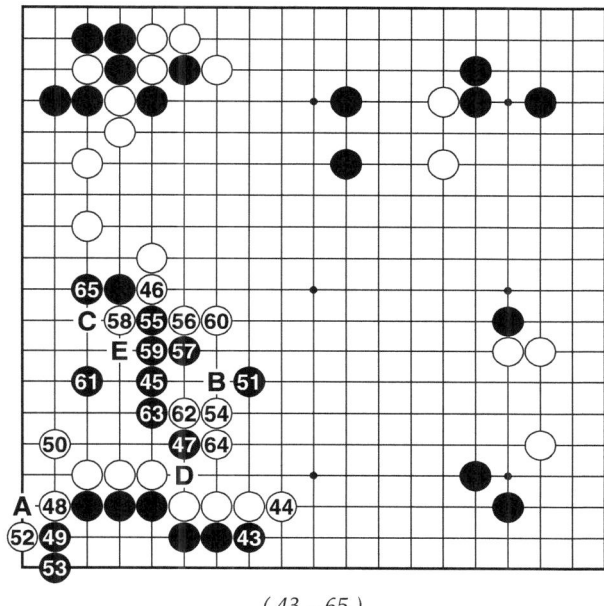

(43 – 65)

43 This push on the second line ensures that the corner is alive, even when the exchange 48 to 50 is played. Furthermore, Black wants to prevent a sente move at 43 for White.

50 A good technique. Black has no time to protect the corner with a move at A, as White will start attacking Black's stones with B. Black 43 allows for leaving the corner as it is and playing in the center first.

51 AI would prefer to play 55 immediately.

60 This is a difficult decision: whether to play territory-oriented at C or focused on the center like in the game. In this situation, AI gives a slight preference to the territorial move.

61 Not a mistake. However, Black at 62 could be considered as well. This move forces White to connect at D and keeps the route open into the center. Then, if White tries to secure the edge with a move at 61, Black simply answers at E.

65 Black is cut off from the center, but managed to live within White's sphere. At this point White is ahead by about four points, and he has sente.

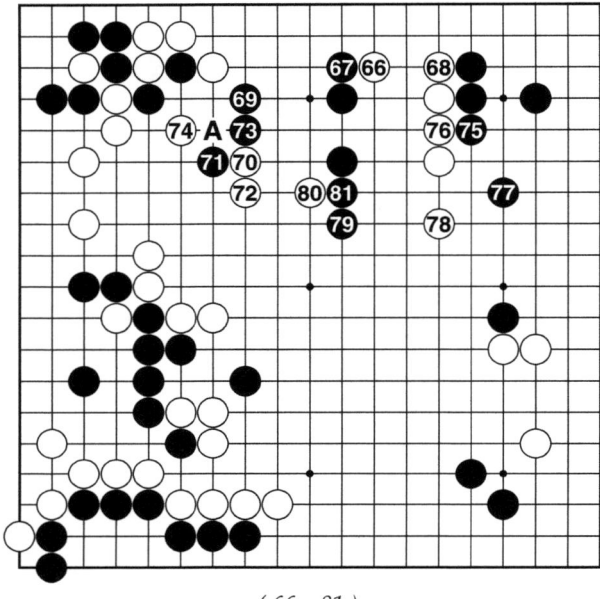

(66 – 81)

66 White prevents Black from connecting at the edge and thus starts a running battle. Neither group has a base yet.

71 This is a strong response to the attack of White 70. White can neither push in at 73 nor hane at A. In both scenarios the stone at 70 becomes separated, in one even captured.

75 After Black's group in the top center has created a base, Black takes territory on the right hand side while forcing White to run.

79 Black cannot allow a white capping move at this point. After this jump it becomes more difficult for White to make territory in the center.

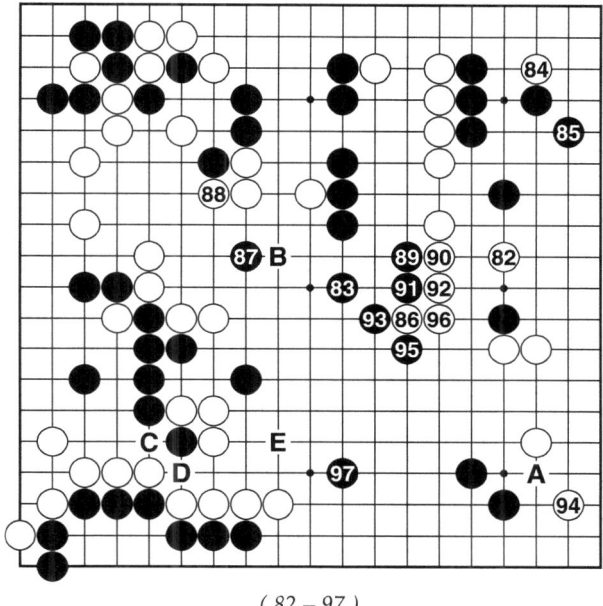

(82 – 97)

84 A probe. Black has to defend to prevent White from creating a living position in the corner.

87 Black A would be a big move here. However, the move in the game is forcing, as it threatens to capture three of White's center stones. Black has to defend at 88 because cutting with B doesn't work.

89 Black is pressing with 89 to 91 against White's stones in order to stabilize his own group in the center by making eye shape.

94 A big move.

97 This move aims at making territory not only at the bottom, but also in the center. After the exchange of C for D, Black could surround the area with E.

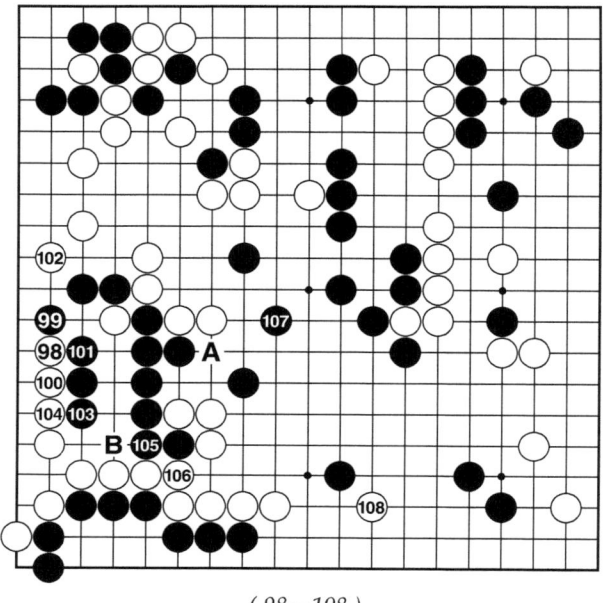

(98 – 108)

98   Shin spent almost ten minutes of his time to continue with 98.

102   The moves at 105 and at 102 are miai.

107   Black must be careful. If White cuts at A he is forced to make life
for his group. Black must be prepared to have a secure way out
when White starts destroying the eye shape with B.

108   A deep invasion. A more
calm way to continue is
shown in the variation,
where White takes
advantage of sente moves
against Black's group on
the left side before aiming
at the big endgame moves
A and B.

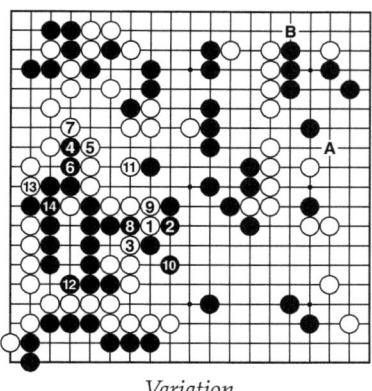

Variation

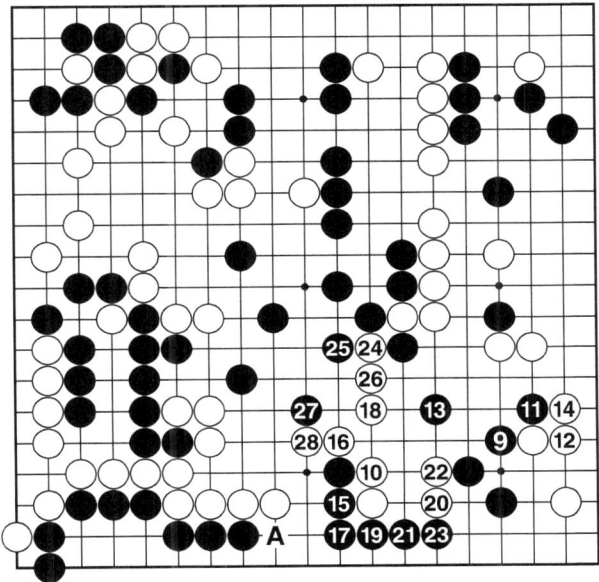

(*109 – 128*)

109 Black cannot capture the invading stone because there is still an escape route to the left side, as shown in the variation. If Black hanes at 6, White will play hane and connect at 5, threatening to link up along the edge. The three of Black's stones would be weakened as well.

115 Black has played 109 to 113 to block White's escape route. Still, it seems he cannot capture the two white stones with 15.

123 Black is crawling on the second line to link up his stones.

124 This cut splits Black's groups. If White also gets A then all three of Black's groups have to make life independently.

128 A calm defensive move. White has built a lead of about seven points.

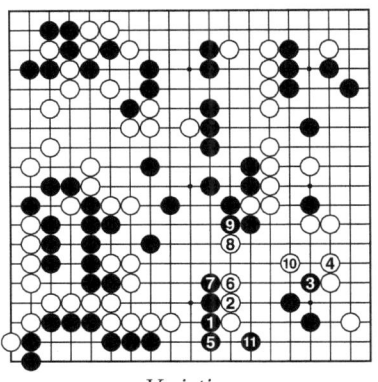

Variation

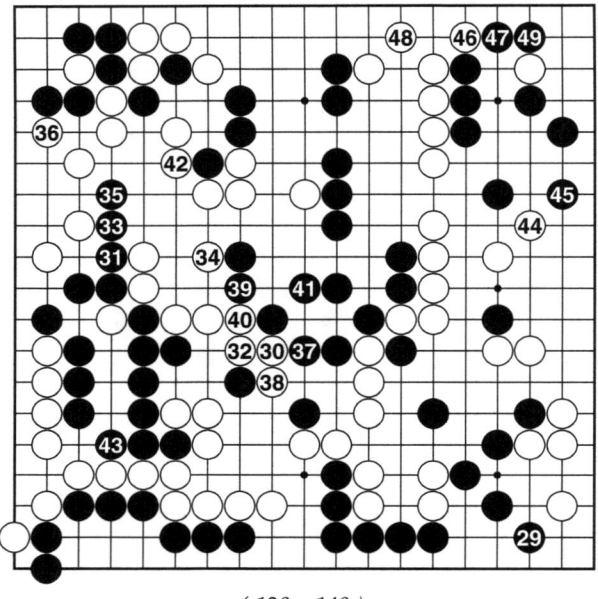

(129 – 149)

130 White aims at the weaknesses in Black's position.

131 Black counters with the push.

132 Blocking at 133 is risky for White, so he aims for a trade.

136 This move protects against a cut by Black.

143 Finally, Black must make life for his group.

144 The game enters the stage of endgame with White still having a good lead of about six points.

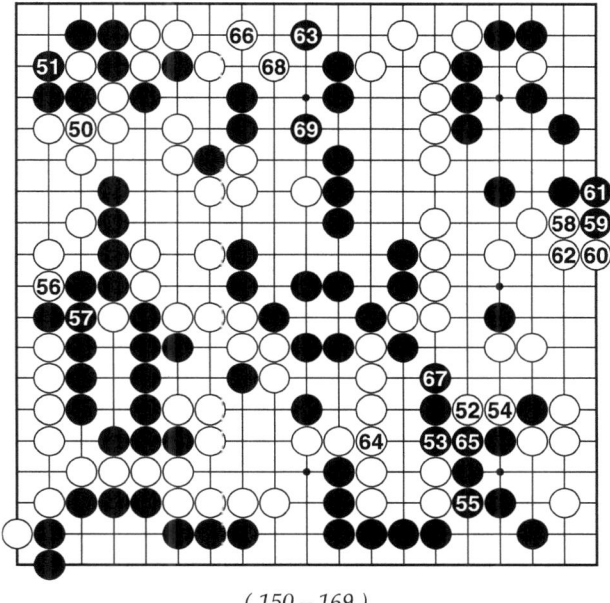

(*150 – 169*)

150 While the game proceeds with the endgame, Park Junghwan's face reveals more and more a loss in faith that there will be an opportunity to gain enough points to win this final game.

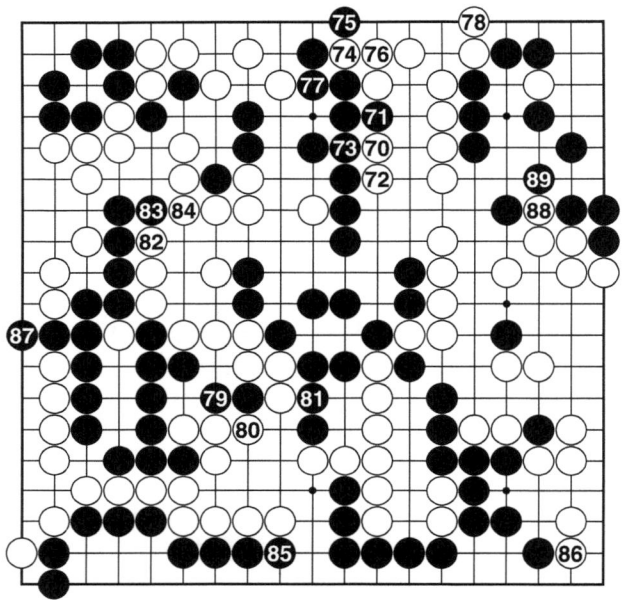

(170 – 189)

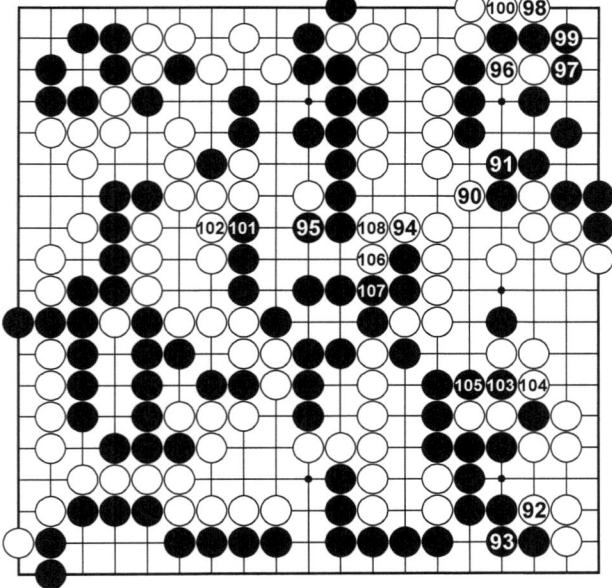

(190 – 208)

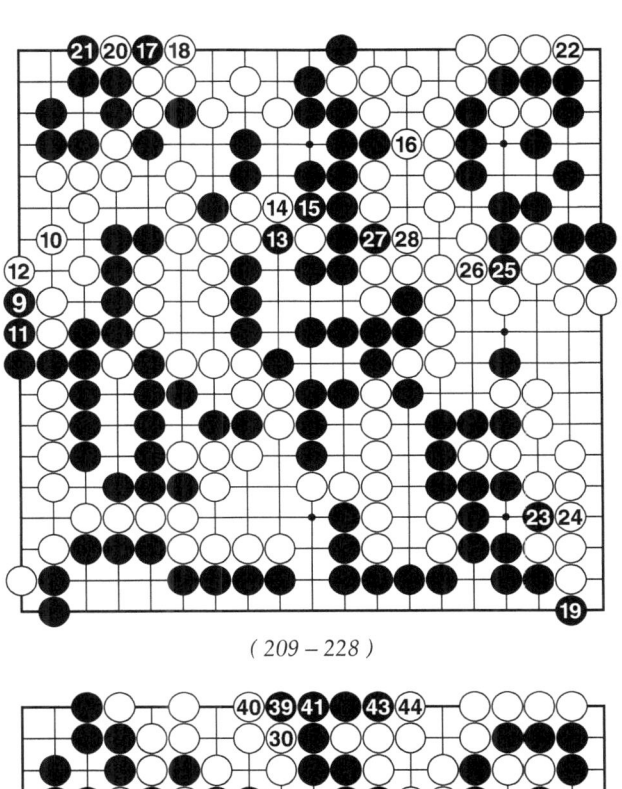

(209 – 228)

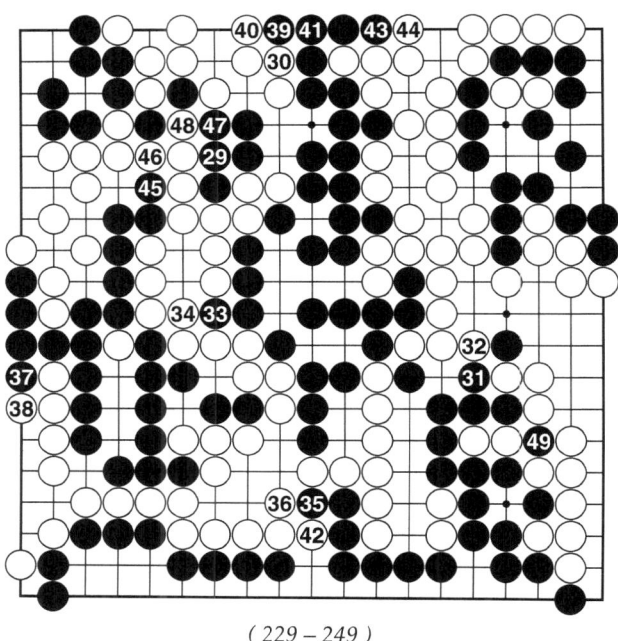

(229 – 249)

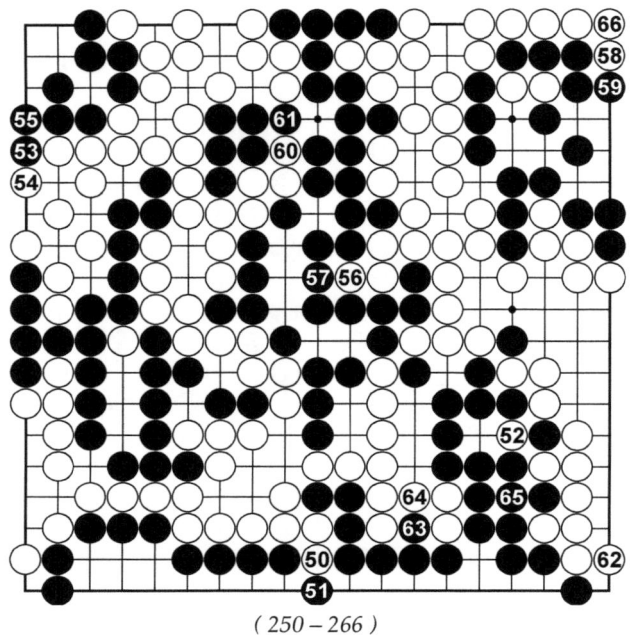

(250 – 266)

266 Park sees no chance to reverse White's lead and resigns.

With this amazing 7-0 win against Park Junghwan in the Namhae Super Match, Shin Jinseo confirmed his rank as „Number One" in Korea. It's the beginning of his era, promising a lot of exciting games.

ANNEX

● **Park Junghwan** ○ **Shin Jinseo**

Date: 2020/07/27
Game: 3rd Korean Yongseong, second final
Time: fisher time; 20 minutes per player and 20 seconds
given per move.
Komi: 6.5

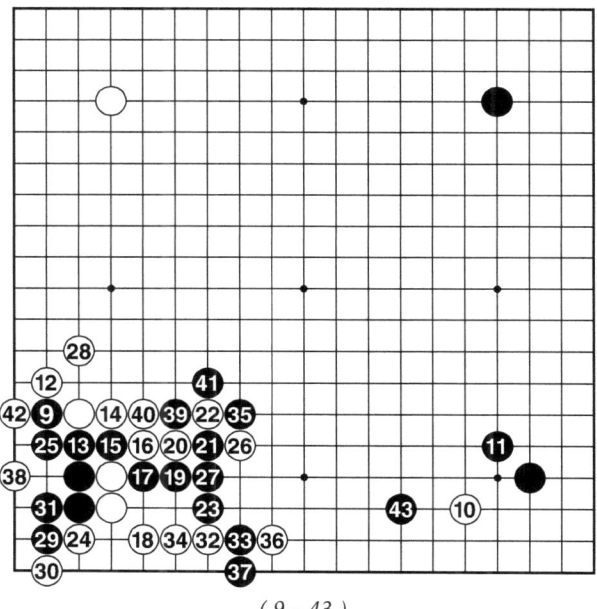

(9 – 43)

This game shows a variation of the Flying Dagger Joseki, played earlier the same year between Park Junghwan and Shin Jinseo. Here, it is Shin Jinseo making the offer with the keima in the lower left corner. Park attached at 9, allowing White to play 12 and 14 which form the entrance into this particular joseki.

This game ended with a score of 0.5 points for Shin, winning him the title of the 3rd Korean Yongseong.

YAMADA SHINJI

HOW TO PLAY GO THE **AI WAY**!

Explained with illustrative diagrams

This book is intended for amateurs in go who would like to learn and employ the modern AI style. The AI style may seem confusing because there are so many tactics far away from traditional thinking. But the study of the new techniques introduced by AI has already lead to their rapid spread and adoption. Today they are applied by pros almost as a matter of course.

This book summarizes the findings from the study of AI techniques and explains them with illustrative diagrams.

„I wrote this book with a lot of enthusiasm and I hope that this way everybody can profit from the insights of my studies. I am very happy to be able to witness this important turning point towards a new era, in which an AI can defeat humans in the game of go. Engaging with the AI style has given me joy like I have never felt before in go. I hope this kind of joy will be conveyed and passed on through the book.“ Yamada Shinji 6p

ISBN 978-3-940563-40-8

2020, 196 pages

BOARD N'STONES